Wind and Birds and Human Voices

Ellen Wilbur

Wind and Birds and Human Voices
and other stories

STUART WRIGHT, *Publisher*

Acknowledgments

I wish to express my thanks to the editors of the following publications in which these stories first appeared:

THE GEORGIA REVIEW: *Wind and Birds and Human Voices*
NEW LETTERS: *Three Vignettes*
PLOUGHSHARES: *Perfection; Ned*
SHENANDOAH: *Wealth*
THE VIRGINIA QUARTERLY REVIEW: *Faith*

With gratitude to the Ingram Merrill Foundation; to my family; to Pam Edwards, Stratis Haviaras, Dewitt Henry, Fanny Howe, Katiti Jean-Baptiste, Bernard and Jane McCabe, Kent Nelson, and Eugene Pool. With loving thanks to my brother, Chris, for his brilliant editorial eye, and to George Garrett for his fire, his humor, his enthusiasm, and his selfless help and great encouragement to so many aspiring writers, this one included.

First Edition

for Peter

Contents

This Consciousness that is aware
Of Neighbors and the Sun
Will be the one aware of Death
And that itself alone

Is traversing the interval
Experience between
And most profound experiment
Appointed unto Men—

How adequate unto itself
Its properties shall be
Itself unto itself and none
Shall make discovery.

Adventure most unto itself
The Soul condemned to be—
Attended by a single Hound
Its own identity.

                    Emily Dickinson

Wind and Birds and Human Voices

Sundays

SHE COULDN'T REMEMBER when he'd started lying down on Sunday afternoons. He hadn't done it when they first were married. At least not regularly. Now he seemed to do it every week, each Sunday sometime after four. She'd notice the sudden quiet in the house when he lay down, but then she would forget it, lost in some task. She'd be wiping down the woodwork, washing windows, sweeping up the hall or cooking, humming to herself and peaceful in the way she only felt when she was busy. Of all the days she liked Sundays the best. The other days went by so fast, they jumbled all together. But Sunday was long. The hours passed slowly, with dignity, like time out of her childhood. She could catch up on things she'd missed or put off all the week while she was out at work. She liked to bake on Sundays. She made pies and home-made breads or muffins. All the things he liked. She'd prepare a roast of lamb or beef or chicken with potatoes. The kitchen windows steamed up in the winter and the cooking smells spread through the whole of the little house until it was so warm and homey that it seemed to cry out for the child they'd lost, the tiny girl who'd lived only one day, whose perfect little face was still so real to her that when she thought of it her hand would fly up to her mouth, and she would sometimes throw the kitchen door wide open to the chill and let the frigid air pour into the cheerful, steamy room.

It always took her by surprise to find him lying down. She'd be carrying up the laundry or her sewing when she'd pass the open bedroom door and see him on their bed. Sometimes she'd hurry past the door without a word as if the sight of him embarrassed her. She couldn't imagine lying down during the day doing nothing. Just the thought of it made her jumpy. If he'd only sleep, it

1

wouldn't bother her so much. But he never did. He lay there wide awake and he looked unlike himself. Sometimes not even gazing out the window, but staring up at the empty ceiling in a way that made her think of someone very old. Yet he was only thirty-five, a burly, lively man. He looked out of place, lying so still.

Why shouldn't the poor man rest, she told herself. He worked hard all week long. He was up before her every morning, wide awake the moment that he rose. She'd wake to the sound of him whistling in the shower and have to wrench herself up through a wall of sleep and hurry down to fix his breakfast. She'd have his orange juice fresh squeezed, his eggs done over light, his dark rye lightly buttered and his coffee steaming in his cup by the time he appeared with his briefcase in his hand.

"I don't know why you make yourself get up. I could just as easily eat out," he'd said hundreds of times. She didn't have to be at work till ten.

She stood at the window when he left the house. He liked to walk the mile down town to catch the train to work. Even in winter he went off through ice or heavy snow as if the weather couldn't touch him. He had a light, springy walk for someone so large. She'd never seen another man who walked exactly as he did.

He never watched t.v. or listened to the radio or read when he lay down on Sundays. His stillness and his silence fascinated her. When they went out to parties, people hurried up to greet him. They gathered all around him. He was such a talker and a story teller. She was shy in groups. She never laughed or joked or became close to people at her job the way he did. He was always calling her to see if he could bring somebody home to supper. Yet when they were alone together, he was quiet. She did most of the talking, as if there were no end to all the things she'd like to tell him.

"Tom?" she said some Sundays, stopping at the bedroom door. He'd turn and look at her with a little smile, never startled. He wasn't a nervous man, not at all like her. "What were you thinking about just then? You looked a million miles away." She doors. It was the first time he'd been outside in years. I could see that he was delighted. It wasn't long before he wanted to go out every day regardless of the weather.

The hospital grounds are enormous. They are gorgeously planted and meticulously gardened. Never have you seen such giant, spreading elms that look like great explosions in the air, or such luxurious lawns of grass so darkly green and thick. There are so many paths, long lanes planted with rows and rows of flowers, all of them perfect. You never see a dead one. "Think of the expense," I've said to Henry. "And who is it for?" Most of the patients never leave the buildings. When we take our daily walks, we rarely see a soul. I push the Baron ahead of me in his chair. His eyes are as good as mine. There is nothing wrong with his hearing or his sense of smell. He enjoys the view the same as I do.

A change came over me as I began to spend my time with Henry Baron. I no longer played cards with the day nurse, Mrs. Cooley. Nor did I shoot the breeze with the attendant, Arthur Little, who'd used to walk the corridors with me and smoke, discussing tennis tournaments and football scores nights when I couldn't sleep. I stopped talking to everyone but Henry. When I was asked a question, I didn't answer it. Mrs. Cooley kept after me at first, and Arthur made it difficult, too. "What's the matter, Paul?" they'd say. "Are you angry? Are you depressed?" But after a while they let me be.

It was a relief to talk to no one but the Baron. It was such a relief that I wrote a letter to my family and I asked them not to visit me for a while. I knew my brother Bill would be happy to receive this news. He'd just been made the president of his company. The more successful he's become, the harder it's been for him to visit me. In his three-piece suit and his white Buick he arrives, his hair still thick and tousled, but now grey, his face a mask of shame when I ask about his work, his pretty wife Melina, who sends me cards for every holiday, and their three children, one of whom is named for me. Bill thinks I must be envious of him. My mother, frail and in her seventies, would be spared the hour of strain in the hospital, a nightmare world through which she's always walked with carefully averted eyes. Behind her cheerful, powdered face I've always felt the misery of her love escape and float across to me as strong as her perfume. My sister, Kathleen, who lives nearby, two towns away, is a social worker, recently divorced from her husband Michael after twenty years. They were never able to have children, which is the disappointment of Kathleen's life. She's overworked and haggard looking now. Her face is colorless and deeply lined. No matter how fond she's always been of me, I knew she too would feel released when I told her I wasn't up to having visitors.

I hadn't known him long before I sensed that Henry and I were kindred creatures with a surprising amount in common. Not just two mental patients bound by our afflictions. I believed that he had been and continued to be a man of sophistication and intelligence. It is intriguing how much you can learn about a man without his ever uttering a word. I sat beside his bed. The sun shone on the white spread, the stiff sheets, and on his hands which lay at his sides with the palms turned up as if to catch the light. The Baron's hands always surprised me. They seemed so large for a man his size. The fingers were long and tapering, delicate and white, the hands of a philosopher or an artist. While I spoke, he listened, staring at the ceiling. Sometimes when he turned to look at me there was such sympathy in his eyes, I felt I could see the whole expression of his face beneath the bandages. Our friendship had changed him too. He no longer wept. Some nights, sensing he was awake, I slipped down the hall to check on him. Often I found him gazing out the window at the moonlit sky. But he seemed completely calm and I felt as proud as if his mood were my accomplishment. In fact I saw a vast improvement in him, a rising of his spirits, and an exuberance that seemed to build, as if he were coming more to life each day. He looked forward to our walks with an eagerness that touched me. Out of doors on a particularly pretty afternoon or evening when the air was pulsing with bird cries or drifting with the fragrance of pine or flowers or fresh mown grass, he would sometimes stop the chair, throw up his hands and hold them up or out in front of him as if he couldn't contain his enthusiasm and would have liked to embrace the whole view for all the beauty he saw in it. Whenever he did this, I felt a peculiar stab of pain, as if the memory of joy, of fearless and ecstatic praise were more than I could bear; I, who always expected the worst.

I saw that Henry was a passionate man. He reminded me of myself, the person I'd used to be so long ago that I could hardly call it myself any longer. I was certain that his rapture would not last, that the novelty of my company and the out-of-doors would wear out. Then, having tasted happiness, I was sure he would like all men be hungry for more. But how much could the Baron hope for? What kind of a life? I expected that eventually, any day now, he would fall into a cavernous depression. I told myself I'd regret that I'd ever spoken with him. But I continued to see him every day.

In the spring we started to play chess. In the morning we'd have a game, usually in Henry's room. He never liked to sit in the dayroom. The sight of the other patients pacing or babbling to themselves or staring off in space depressed him. I was surprised he hadn't gotten used to it. Also the television which is always on. The sound of it got on his nerves. And the bad air. Even in summer with the windows open there is a strong smell, a sour human smell. Not to mention all of the cigarette smoke. Being a smoker myself, it never bothered me. But Henry was always happiest when we were by ourselves and out-of-doors. As the weather grew warmer, we took our game outside. There was a picnic table under a large maple tree at the back of our building. The Baron sat in his chair. I sat on the bench across from him, and no one ever bothered us. If I'd had any doubts about the Baron's mind or whether his reasoning ability had been impaired, they were put to rest when I saw him play chess. He was a slow but ingenious player, with enormous concentration. There wasn't a move he made that wasn't deeply calculated, and in the end he always trounced me.

Often I'd stop in the middle of a game and go up to the building to fetch two Cokes from the machine. The smallest things delighted Henry. He gave me the feeling that playing chess and drinking Coke and sitting across from me under the open sky

9

were all that he wanted in the world. When he leaned across the table, shook my arm, and smiled with all-out pleasure, it was as if he had no memory of suffering or injury, as if he had no past at all. It was strange how much his happiness, even the smallest evidence of it, affected me with pride, anxiety and even fear, and the more inseparable we became, the more I seemed to feel the power of his personality as if it were the atmosphere I breathed.

One afternoon, after Henry had played a brilliant game, we stayed at the table. The day was warm and the air so fresh it rose and danced for miles above, as if the winter sky had been a heavy roof that now was lifted. There was a soaring, endless feeling to the air. His head resting on one hand, Henry gazed at the view. His eyes appeared to be completely serene. I found myself staring at him, wondering what his problem was and why they'd put him on the psychiatric ward. There's little mystery about our chronics. Most of them have been here years. You know their fears and their obsessions as well as you'd know a normal man's opinions. I stared at Henry. His physical disability, his deformity, was obvious, but other than his initial fits of weeping, I'd seen no signs of his psychosis. Not once in the five months he'd been on the ward. Of course, I, too, had been unusually well the whole time I had known him. I wondered if, like me, his illness had a cycle. Like me and Ben Dimento who fought in Viet Nam. My cycle used to be as regular as Ben's. Six months of perfect health, six months of hell. Like clockwork. The doctors used to study me. I've read about myself in psychiatric journals. I wondered if the Baron was like me, if even now behind that calm facade he felt the signs, the subtle stirrings of his illness, as if it were a hibernating giant, half-roused by sounds and smells of spring. There wasn't a summer since the war when I hadn't been completely mad.

I studied Henry closely, whose upturned face still looked so satisfied. I thought of the way he relied on me more and more. He waited for me anxiously every morning. When I appeared, he took my arm with pleasure and relief. His growing dependence was flattering, but it worried me, sometimes to the point where my hands trembled when I thought of it. When Henry noticed the trembling, he sometimes took my hands in his and held them until the shaking stopped. He took my hands so naturally and with such ease, there was no embarrassment in it. I felt that I must warn him and prepare him for the worst, but I couldn't bring myself to do it yet.

II.

When I think of my past, the early happy years are another life, a story that came to an end as final and complete as death. The child I was is a stranger about whom I know everything, a boy named Paul who showed an interest in the piano. When he'd come in from school, this little Paul would go straight to the living room, which in the afternoon was orderly and hushed. The sun poured silently through gleaming windows down on the spotless, yellow carpet, and the air was faintly scented with his father's pipe tobacco. He'd pass the flowered couch, the tables rubbed with lemon oil to shining, and slide across the slippery bench before the looming upright Steinway whose heavy ivory keys lay waiting, faintly yellowed to a color which seemed sanctified with mystery and beauty. Often he'd start to play with his hat and coat still on and stay there till his mother ordered him outside for an hour of fresh air. When he was six, he started lessons, and from that moment was so enchanted and possessed that had he been allowed he would have done nothing else but play. In the evenings after dinner he'd go back to practice. His father, if he were at home, would puff his pipe and read in his high-backed chair across the room. "That's *wonderful*, Paul," he'd sometimes say with real surprise. He had no musical ability himself and was slightly awed by the reports of the piano teacher, Adele Archer, who said she'd never had a pupil with such promise. His mother, too, was pleased, but not surprised. She seemed to expect her children would do wonders and was only amazed when they were rude or bad.

He learned to play his little Bach and Mozart pieces easily, played them over till the lurching notes smoothed together and rang out proudly from his hands. By the time he was eight he began to give recitals with several of Miss Archer's other pupils. He sat before a crowd without the slightest nervousness or fear, and while he played a silence louder than applause would build within the room inspired by the confidence and the natural bravado with which the child performed.

Throughout those early years Miss Archer's long horse face appeared to be continually wreathed with admiration. At their weekly lessons she listened to him play, her hands clasped tight against her chest, as if a miracle were happening in her living room. "It is *astonishing* the way he picks up everything so quickly," she told his parents in a voice that nearly trembled, her face becoming radiant when she looked down at her kindled student whose future rose before her like the sun. "I've been waiting for a child like Paul for thirty years," she said.

Something about Adele Archer's flushed cheeks, the long strands of her hair which came unpinned in her excitement and hung disheveled by her face, disturbed the father. The careless look of her clothes, the way her skirts hung on her bony frame, and the surprising feeling in her naked eyes, gave her a starved, unhealthy look. "I worry about that woman," he'd sometimes say to the mother in a burst of impatience. "I think she's pushing the boy too hard."

But it wasn't Miss Archer who drove Paul to practice longer and longer hours. It was the music, the subtlety and the difficulty of it which steadily increased, as if he'd been continually climbing, had passed the easy foothills and now found himself upon a startling slope which rose up with a steepness that required all of his skill. By the time he was twelve he began to dream of mountains, soaring alps which stretched before him in a chain of glory all the way to the horizon, each mountain higher than the last. The farthest peaks towards which he struggled were lost in clouds of unimaginable beauty.

One night, after a recital, Dr. Winslow, a friend of his father's, came up to congratulate him. "Tell me, Paul. What would you do if you couldn't play the piano anymore?" he said with a teasing smile. The question hung in the air while the child's face twisted with confusion. "I would die," he said at last, and he saw his own dismay reflected in the doctor's face.

Paul liked it best to practice in the summer, sunny days when his mother opened all the windows and the out-of-doors hummed like a great machine. From where he sat he had a view of his mother's terraced garden. Often she worked with her flowers or his father would appear at the door of the tool shed, the sun flashing in his glasses, and a world of sounds and smells rode through the room. He played to the noise of voices, footsteps, birds, and the steady whine of insects, as if the sounds of summer were his orchestra. And when he played his best, he disappeared into the music, drifted on the notes right out the window of the lonely room into the brilliant summer yard, rose above the buildings, moved in the heavy laden trees, or wafted out across the grass with an intensity that made his mother put her trowel down and turn to stare at the dark empty window.

After summer came dim afternoons when rain pelted the windows and the wind blew hard and wild outside while the room remained untouched. And winter days when the sky was a heavy, shifting veil of grey and the snow descended hour after hour, steadily and slowly, until the piano sounded loud and harsh in the vast accumulating silence. There were evenings when his concentration built like such an all-surrounding wall, it was a great relief to turn away from the piano, to find his mother knitting on the couch behind him, to see the colors of her sweater, pink or mauve or emerald green, and all the colors of the room leap forward with surprising brightness like a welcome. He'd rise with a sudden feeling of exhaustion, go to sit by his mother's feet, rest his head against her knee, and gaze into the cheerful, blazing fireplace like a traveler returning from a distance. He'd stare at the steadfast lamps and chairs and tables, feel the warmth of the fire and of his mother's love which flowed through the hand she placed on his shoulder, and he'd stay there till the sense of lostness, separateness had passed.

Already he'd felt the power of his mind, the way it could bewitch and hold him captive, lost to the world while his hands ran up and down the keys, enchanted little hands that moved so

13

freely, of their own volition. And the more he disappeared into the music, the more important grew the moment when he'd turn away from the piano to face the solid beauty of the room. He came to count upon the impact of the room as if it were a healing blow that broke a spell releasing him from his mind back to the world. Years later, when he'd come home for a weekend visit, when he'd wander through the house as if he needed to inspect the rooms, he would avoid the living room. Home from the hospital for a long weekend, he'd climb the staircase to the second floor, follow the trail of rugs along the hall and stop at each open bedroom door. He'd tour the grounds, pause by his mother's garden, pass through the long dark dining room into the commotion of the kitchen or sit long hours on the veranda or the porch. But he never would go near the living room. The family was sure it must be the piano he avoided, that the sight of it was devastating to him. But they were wrong. It wasn't the piano, but the living room itself he couldn't bear to see, because it, too, had lost all impact, any power to bring him back, and now appeared, like all the world, to be a dream.

III.

I have no memories of the war. Perhaps the heavy drugs I've taken have destroyed them. Whole years are gone as if they had been bombed into oblivion. I'm told that I saw action only for six months and that my company was at Anzio when I was declared mentally incompetent and unfit and shipped home to a psychiatric hospital. I remember little of the two years that I spent at Glenside Hospital. Only that I was disoriented and that my doctor discouraged me from playing the piano because it caused me too much stress. I was told that my prognosis was good and that with patience, time, and rest I would recover. I never believed this. In fact my weekend visits home convinced me I was growing steadily worse. I was twenty and I saw the world with the detachment and nostalgia of a dying man. All the most normal events and common sights developed poignancy and power. A table set for five became poetic. An easy chair, a rug, a pair of shoes, the faithful stars, the rising sun all developed extra meaning and importance. The world became a place of shining warmth within which normal people lived entirely immersed. I'd see them walking down the street at home with every shape or shade of color, temperature or change of weather, basking in familiar sounds and smells, unsurprised by anything. I'd see the way these people blindly ate their meals, conversed and sipped their drinks or calmly slept with an acceptance that made all human weaknesses and failings appear harmless and endearing for the innocence implied by such enormous faith, a faith which made a man belong entirely to the world the way a thoughtless tree belongs. While I, as I became more ill, became more outcast, saw all life with a clarity and distance which shattered innocence, with the loneliness of a voyeur who feels the shame of his detachment as if it were the greatest sin of all. Sometimes I was so overcome with consciousness that I could not remember how to hold a fork or walk across a room with any ease or grace.

Each summer there is a day when a trumpet blast cuts through the air. Then, if I strain my ears, I can hear the faintest sound of beating drums, the distant tramp of soldier's feet, and the rattle of their sabers. I can hear an army marching far away but on its way to me. It is a sound which used to chill my blood. In the early years I'd pace the floor for weeks while the steady tramp of feet grew louder. I'd moan, I'd cry, I'd pull my hair and beat my head against the floor until they'd have to put restraints on me. "Save me," I'd beg the orderlies and nurses. They'd look at me with pity and they'd drug me heavily, but nothing stopped the steady pounding feet which grew continually louder. Sometimes I passed out from the strain or fell into a swoon of fear on the hard floor. I'd see the hospital for days bathed in a brilliant shade of pink, then darkening to an ever deeper red until the nurses and the other patients all began to fade slowly and horribly. At last they disappeared in darkness.

Each year this sequence of events repeats itself with a hundred variations. Once the hospital has faded out I remain in a darkness more profound and deep than any in the living world. The stomp of feet is deafening by now and the rat-tat-tat of drums. I wait for the moment of total silence which comes just at the instant when I least expect it, that moment when the drums cease, when the feet come to a sudden halt, and when there is a rolling, awesome quiet more powerful than any sound. How long this pregnant silence lasts, this final moment of transition, I can't say. I wait in that hopeless blackness which is timeless.

Some years, at the boom of a single cannon, a scene completely formed bursts in a bloom of color all around me. I'm sure I'll never know the meaning of this stark, familiar scene, this panoramic grand display of symbols crucial to my soul. I stand at the edge of a skeletonic forest which has been entirely destroyed by fire. Before me lies a scorched field two miles wide which rises to a distant pointed ridge. All across this lifeless field the grass is blackened to the ground. No birds appear here, no brave surviving squirrel roots in the broken stubble of the forest. Not even the lowest insect lives or moves in this still landscape. I search the view, hoping to find some hole in it, some weakness of imagination which will make it less believable. But everything I see is starkly real and rendered perfectly down to the last detail of distance and perspective. The more I look, the more the overwhelming authenticity of the scene wraps and seals itself around me in such a way that there is no escape.

Some years I see the army marching toward me over that conquered field with all the glamour of a history painting come to life in the smoky, hazy light. I see how antiquated their weapons are, all their swords, their cannons and equipment, as if this army had defeated time itself. The faces of the men are hard and white, their uniforms a brilliant red with yellow tassels at the shoulders, fringe along the sleeves. The boots they wear are shiny, black and high.

Sometimes I see the General himself who leads them on a skittish, prancing horse, his thick straight hair tossed back from his enormous, chisled face, his eyes steely and harsh above a twisted, cruel mouth. He rarely speaks to me as he approaches. He doesn't need to speak. He leads his men into my consciousness each summer. He plants the flag of his possession deep and makes my mind his camping place.

Some years I never see the men at all, but I know exactly how they look. The taste of them is like the taste of metal in my mouth. And it is suffering, pain enough to feel the bruising touch of all their striding, heedless feet. A mind is sacred ground. You cannot know this till the moment of a great invasion. You cannot know the awful pressure or the frightful strain as the men file in, toss all their weapons down and the heavy weight of their equipment. Yet still they keep arriving, pressing in until there isn't any inch of empty space left in me, and the tidal sound of them, the roaring chaos and the grand confusion of them rises to a pitch that shatters my last desperate concentration. Then I am nothing. I am theirs.

When I was first at Washington V.A., I used to fight each onset of my illness. At the sound of the trumpet blast in June, I picked up chairs and heaved them all the way across the dayroom. I broke windows. I put my fist through the television screen. The more I fought the more enormous my strength grew. One year I took on the whole cafeteria. I threw plates and trays. I flipped the trestle tables over and I flung them in the air light as balloons. I picked up cups and smashed them one by one against the ceilings, floors, and walls. No one could stop me. It took six orderlies to bring me down. They had to lock me in a padded cell from June to Christmas. I was a holy terror in those days. But the army was equally impressive. The men were young and fresh, invincible and fierce. They had no wounds or scars or any sign of weakness. Their uniforms were new and spotless, made of such a brilliant red it hurt the eyes to look at them.

They spoke to me. For half the year I heard their voices, loud and scornful, cold and haughty, or soft and silky and insinuating. Sometimes they spoke to me in choruses, in waves, and sometimes singly, individually using whatever tone was most effective at the time. I lay on a mat on the floor of my padded cell. The walls were white. One naked bulb hung down protected by a wire cage eight feet above. Their voices, dark and predatory, circled me, and in those days there was no end to the havoc they could cause.

Two weeks before my father died, he tried to visit me. Maybe he had a premonition of his heart attack. My mother drove up to the hospital with him. They came one afternoon just after lunch. The doctors wouldn't let them see me. I was far too ill for visitors, they were told. Of course nobody let me know that my parents had arrived. I was sitting in a chair on the ward, staring off in space, when something made me rise and walk across the room to the right window. I looked down at the parking lot and was surprised to see my father and mother walking to their car. It was warm. The window was barred, but it was open. I was going to call down to them. I was just about to when I saw my father stop. His face was in his hands. He was bent over, and my mother put her arm around his waist. She seemed to be supporting him. They looked so small, I felt I could have picked them up and held them in my hand. The cloudless sky was blue and vast above them and for just that moment I could truly see what I had done to them. Many times I have imagined and replayed this scene. My parents are in the parking lot with all the joy, the life gone out of them and I am at the high-barred window unable to call down to them. Did it ever really happen? I am never sure.

Some rare, cool-headed nights when I was in my twenties, I used to lie in the purest, soothing darkness of my room at 3 a.m. and glory in the silence of the hospital which seemed to match the quiet of my mind when sanity and privacy had been restored to it. In such a mood of gratitude I'd sometimes have to climb out of my bed, to walk about my room and feel the floor unshakeable and steady under my bare feet. I'd have to touch the metal bed post, to run my hand over the smooth-painted wall, to touch the light switch and to think that if I turned it on I'd see exactly what I would expect to see and nothing more. Sometimes the pleasure and the gratitude were so intense, I'd have to leave my room and step into the lighted hall where the shiny, checked linoleum was all that I saw or wanted to see and where the smudged green walls, the high grey ceilings and the iridescent lights above all waited unobtrusively and humbly, not caring whether I noticed them or not. By four a.m. over the whole ward the silence had a texture thick as soil. On nights like this I'd sometimes ask myself the meaning of my madness the way a normal man might hope to understand the stars or wonder at a stretch of strange, unseasonable weather, as if there had to be some explanation for it. I'd study my own illness with the coldness of a scientist who prides himself on his detachment. I'd ask myself the meaning of the General and the significance of the antiquated army. Why did they come specifically in June, and what was the reason for the six month cycle? Those brave, light-headed nights I'd feel quite sure that if I solved these riddles, my dread army would disintegrate and disappear forever. I'd be cured. But I never found a single answer to my questions. One thing only was clear; that the army's purpose was the purpose of all armies; to demoralize and to defeat the enemy, which was me.

My mother came to see me every year just after Christmas. "How are you, dear?" she'd ask, touching my cheek. "I'm fine," I'd tell her lightly, and I would produce the wide and carefree and preposterous smile I carefully prepared for every meeting with her, which by some miracle of love or mutual collusion was always effective. I saw my mother's face relax. Then we would limp through conversation. There was little to say. In the early years she brought me music scores and books; "The Principles of Composition," and heavy, hard-bound lives of Rimsky-Korsakoff and Charles Ives. I never had the heart to tell her that I could no longer read. I'd lost the concentration for it. "Have you been practicing at all?" she'd ask me hopefully. There was a "music room" in building 9. My first few years at Washington I sometimes practiced on the spinet in that room, though it was always out of tune. But there was never any pleasure in it. Since the war, by some odd twist of heightened nerves and over-sharp perceptions my ear had grown so piercingly acute that I could read a score and hear precisely how a piece should be interpreted down to the finest subtleties of tempo and dynamics. There was a simple Bartok piece I played for weeks hundreds of times a day and never once came close to the perfection of my ear. I went into such fits of fury and frustration banging on the keys that finally I was forbidden from further playing. Dr. Sewell must have spoken to my mother. After that she didn't bring me music anymore. Nor books either. She brought me cartons of the Marlboros I smoked one after another all day long, which were all that I wanted.

Each year, after the army had played out all of their tricks, there came a day in late December when they'd start to pack their gear. I'd watch them break camp in their slow, methodic way. This, too, was torture. It took them days and days. Each year the General came up to me as they were leaving. He came up close until his face was looming and immense. Then he turned his narrowed, knowing eyes hard on me. "You know the rules, Paul," was what he said. "You are to keep everything you've seen and heard here to yourself. One word, one slightest hint of it to anyone and there will be *hell* to pay." Then he mounted his great horse, he whirled away from me, and he was gone. I never wondered at his power, the sinking nausea and the instant terror that the sight of him always inspired. With lips sealed tight as if they had been welded by the General's command, I watched the men file slowly out behind him. It was always raining as they disappeared over the ridge, raining on them and on the muddy ground they'd left all littered and defiled.

I tested the General once, one night of a full moon when I was in my thirties. I started to tell Mrs. Davis, the night nurse, about my army of tormenters. It was a January night. I could see the swollen moon, enormous, cold, and white outside the window of my room. Mrs. Davis was leaning over me, wiping my face with a damp towel. I was lying on my bed. My arms were wrapped with gauze. I'd tried to cut my wrists.

"What is it, Paul?" she said. She could see that I wanted to speak. I took her arm and held it tightly. I planned to tell her everything. And yet when I tried to find words that would describe the army's tactics, and the meaning of those long kaleidoscopic months of nightmare images and darting scenes with which they'd held and punished and absorbed me, my mind appeared to melt into confusion.

"What is it, Paul?" said Mrs. Davis softly. "Can you tell me?" She leaned close over me, over my face which was pouring sweat.

"Try to tell me," she said gently. Her breasts just grazed my chest. A strong perfume came from her. I thought I heard the sound of drums begin, the steady roll and beat of them. I closed my eyes to concentrate and when I opened them I saw that Mrs. Davis was laughing. Her eyes were cruel slits and her white nurse's uniform was turning red. A cry escaped me, but it came out as a trumpet sound, long and high and shrill. I heard the General's voice beside my ear.

"I warned you, Paul," he said. I can remember Mrs. Davis's laughing face, her dress which seemed to float and shimmer red before my eyes, and how I watched her fade until she disappeared in a rising, swimming darkness. That was the last I saw of her for two years. The army kept me raving mad on the locked ward for two years as punishment for my attempted betrayal.

After I came back from that long siege, Bill was the first one in the family to visit me. When they brought me down to the visitor's room, he looked shocked. "You've lost so much weight, Paulie," he said. "You've got to eat more." I asked about Melina and the children and how his work was going. He looked uncomfortable the way he always did when he talked about himself in front of me. I wanted to say "For God's sake, Bill, I'm so far gone you couldn't pay me to be you."

There is a crossing point after long illness when a man begins to dread the possibility of ever being well again more than the prospect of remaining permanently ill. The hospital can recognize the signs; the glassy eyes, the aimless, shambling walk, the robot voice. The empty face without a human sign or message to convey makes a powerful impression, one that might be harmful to the other, healthier patients. This is what the hospital believes and why they've made a special building for the chronics to keep them hidden separate from the others.

When I was forty-two they put me with the chronics. By then it mattered little to me where I lived or slept. In the company of those milling, babbling men who drifted up and down the corridors with the vague directness of sleep-walkers, I sank into a numb obliviousness. Sometimes I was aware that weeks and months had disappeared without my noticing, as if once time had been detached from any purpose, it speeded up and rocketed like something that has been unleashed. Sometimes I watched the clock and felt the pulsing minutes flow unchecked out of my life as swiftly as the rush of blood escaping from a mortal wound.

In the dayroom we sat in chairs against the walls, a long curved row of bodies silent and entranced. The morning sun shone on the floor. It made a yellow square unnoticed and unseen by anyone. In the center of the room a man paced back and forth. All day from his small mouth there came a steady flood of gibberish which rose and fell and was monotonously soothing like the sound of bees.

They didn't have to lock me up in summer anymore. I found this out from Arthur Little. I asked him once whether I was ever violent anymore. "Hell, no, Paul. You're no trouble," he said. "When you're sick, you just sit in your chair all day. You don't talk to nobody and you don't do nothing. You're quiet as a lamb," he said. "Sometimes I walk you up and down the halls to exercise you. Come with me, Paul, is all I have to say. I lead you by the arm and you come right with me. You're no trouble to nobody, Paul," he said. "No trouble at all."

When I turned fifty, I noticed that the General was going grey, and I saw how much all of the men had aged along with me. The company grew slightly smaller every year, and the men appeared less strong and more obviously tired. There were more wounded and more who walked with canes, who limped, and some who had lost an arm or leg. The uniforms were soiled and patched. The boots were worn. Some had no boots and walked with painful feet bound up with cloth and tape. As they approached me over the ridge, their faces were more bored than hostile towards me. They rarely spoke to me or wanted my attention. They simply occupied me now. They dressed their wounds and they rested they weary bodies. For the most part they ignored me. One year I noticed that I'd almost lost my fear of them. I even spoke to the General once and I asked him a frivolous question. "You've kept me here all of these years. You've made me suffer any way you could. One thing has always puzzled me," I said. "Why did you let me smoke all of these years? Why did you allow me that one pleasure?"

"Because it was killing you," he replied.

I actually laughed when I heard that, which seemed to dismay the General. For a moment he looked quite shaken, and there was something grotesque about the uncertainty and the frailty I clearly saw in his softened, aging face. Then his expression changed. He smiled.

"I have to admire you, Paul," he said. "You've never betrayed us all of these years." The words were flattering and yet there was a razor tone of irony and scorn in them which made me suddenly look closely at the General's face. At his mouth, which was disdainful and amused. And in his narrowed eyes I saw the confidence and calculation of a player, who, far from finished, still holds a crushing trump card hidden in his hands.

My mother came to see me twice a year, just before the arrival of the army and shortly after their departure, the times I was expected to be well. I don't believe she ever knew how much I had deteriorated. Each time she came onto the ward, I was ready for her, smiling brightly. The nurses must have seen how much these visits cost me. They always warned me several days before my mother came. From whatever depths of illness I had gone to, I heard the nurses' far-off, faintly spoken message, and I would stir and strain to rouse myself from that dim, muffled place of ringing emptiness where I lay hidden and protected. Perhaps it was the place all chronics went to. Then, like a swimmer under heavy weights of water, I would rise to meet my mother on the surface, though the distance and the effort of that passage seemed more onerous each year. Also the pain. The pain of breaking through the surface into the roaring light of the dayroom where the din was overwhelming. I wondered how I ever had endured that brilliant light which bounded sharply off the walls like hurled knives aimed straight at me. And all the world's confusion

23

and commotion. On all sides was shifting, dizzy motion. Such a blast of sharp, intruding smells. I gripped the arms of my hard chair as if I might be shaken free by all the forces in the room. I thought of Mother. I prepared myself to see her.

It was after one of Mother's visits that I first saw Henry Baron. I had walked Mother to the door and was on my way back to the dayroom full of a sense of fatigue so severe that I wondered if I could even make it to my chair. There was a farewell smile still plastered on my face as I passed Henry's room. I never paused. I continued on my way down the long corridor, and yet the image of the man I'd seen stayed right in front of me as if I'd stopped beside his door and still remained there staring at him.

IV.

I arrived at Henry's room by eight o'clock each morning. He no longer liked to take his meals in bed. He enjoyed eating with me. I always found him wide awake and waiting eagerly for my arrival. His eyes lit up and shone with happiness when I appeared at his door. It is hard to describe the effect that this greeting had on me. I was not used to bringing joy to anybody. But then I was not used to any of the changes in my life since I'd known Henry. Often it seemed impossible that he was sitting across from me, that I'd just spoken to him. I kept expecting him to disappear. I was quite sure that some fine day I'd find his bed made up and empty. He'd be gone as suddenly as he'd come, and there would be no explanation for it. Perhaps the Baron had this same anxiety and that was why he greeted me with such enthusiasm every morning. He grasped my hand and held it tightly. Then I helped him into his chair and he wheeled himself down to the cafeteria where we had our breakfast. While we ate, we often planned what we would do that day. In the mornings we played chess or we sat together dozing in the sun. Hours would go by without a word or sign exchanged between us, yet there was a constant feeling of communion of a kind I'd never known with anyone before. It frightened me.

I could now sit comfortably in the morning sun. The light was soft. It wasn't painful to my eyes. I could look across the rolling lawn of shifting grass and swaying trees and passing cars without the slightest dizziness. Clouds inched across the sky, birds flew, and people walked among the buildings while I remained un-moved, perfectly still. The morning sounds of droning mowers, gardener's clippers, wind and birds and human voices seemed subdued and gentle to my ears.

I stopped playing cards with Mrs. Cooley. To sit with her seemed tiresome and pointless. In fact all talk with anyone but Henry was annoying. When I wrote my family not to visit me, I was surprised at how pleased I felt. More amazing was the tre-mendous improvement in my thinking the moment I stopped speaking with the staff. The very day I broke communications with them, my concentration sharpened to a point where I came very close to beating Henry at chess. My mind was suddenly so clear that I could see the fuzzy, muddying effect that my twice-daily dose of medications had on it. I began to hide the pills they gave me underneath my tongue and to dispose of them whatever way I could. In the days that followed, as I grew increasingly alert and energetic, it came as an unpleasant shock to think that all the drugs I'd swallowed since the war might have done more harm than good.

In the afternoons we took our walks. We headed down the path and the row of ominous brick buildings shrank behind us to the size of toys. I pushed the Baron in his chair when he grew tired. Often we went two miles to reach our favorite resting spot. At the top of a steeply winding path was a wide, sheer cliff with a spectacular view of checkered farms far down below. On a grassy knoll above the precipice someone had placed a wooden bench where one could rest and gaze out over the expanse of fields and buildings, woods and lakes, and mountains at the farthest distance. Henry always threw his arms up at the sight of this great liberating view, and I often thought that these wide gestures of his arms, the thousand signals of his delicate long hands and the sharp expressions in his eyes were far more power-fully explicit than words could ever be.

Not far from our cliff view was an old abandoned chapel, a

grey stone building almost hidden in a crowd of juniper and pine. The heavy door was never locked and it was easy to push the Baron's chair over the low sill. More than once we went inside and sat in the silent oblong room of darkly varnished pews and stained glass windows. The air was cut with shafts of purple, red and green and had a musty, piney smell. A wooden cross hung from the wall above the empty marble altar. As we sat in the failing light of afternoon, there was a lonely echo to the bird cries outside of the building and a hollow feeling to the darkening surrounding woods which made me glad that the Baron was beside me.

By early May I felt so well, and I was convinced that all of it was my friend's doing, even the beauty of the Spring and my capacity to perceive it. The sky was a blue pastel day after perfect day. In the balmy warmth and the golden light everything was in bloom. The air that breezed across the grounds was heavily perfumed with lilacs and the banks and banks of lilies, hyacinths and nasturtium which the gardeners daily tended. Beside our building were blonde fountains of forsythia cascading with long sprays of yellow stars. For twenty years or more I'd never noticed spring at all. This year I was intoxicated.

One shadow fell through all of this exhilaration, which was the thought of my approaching army due to arrive in six short weeks or less. They'd always been on schedule. Why wouldn't they be now? And what would Henry think when I no longer showed up in the morning, and when I sat in the dayroom all day long like a vegetable in my chair, as Arthur Little had described it? I could imagine it so well, how Henry, having been so cruelly and inexplicably abandoned, would regress right back to the way he'd been when I first met him. Only this time maybe worse. And perhaps by Christmas when I came back to him, he'd have become unreachable himself. My hands shook when I thought of this. I knew that I must warn my friend and carefully prepare him for our separation, but each day I hesitated.

"I feel so well," I said to him instead, as if the saying of it made it so.

"I feel so amazingly well," I said repeatedly, and Henry nodded that he felt the same.

One morning Mrs. Cooley woke me early. She said she'd made an appointment for me to have a physical examination. Also a dental check. I hadn't been looking well, she thought, and I'd been holding my jaw as if a tooth were bothering me. She'd asked me repeatedly about the tooth as well as my health. Because I wouldn't answer any of her questions she'd felt it her duty to make the appointments for me.

"It won't take long, Paul," she insisted. "You'll feel much better when that tooth is fixed. It *has* been hurting, hasn't it?" she said.

I looked away from her, down at the floor. It was hard not speaking to Mrs. Cooley. I'd always been quite fond of her and thought she had a pleasant manner with the patients. When a man was well enough, she spoke to him as if he were an equal. It hurt me to be rude to her, but I didn't dare to risk it yet. There was no denying the improvement in my head since I had limited all conversation to the Baron.

As I left the ward with Mrs. Cooley, I was tempted to tell Henry where I was going. But it was early, and when I passed his room he was sleeping so soundly that I couldn't bring myself to wake him. I would have liked to leave a message for him with one of the orderlies, but I didn't see how this could be accomplished without talk.

There was a line of patients waiting to see Dr. Barber. I had to wait more than an hour for the physical examination. Outside the window I noticed that the morning had gone dark. The lawn was a sharp, electric green, and black storm clouds were moving swiftly in over the sky with a look of spreading gloom. Mrs. Cooley brought me a cup of coffee and a muffin, but I didn't touch them. I thought of Henry lying in his bed waiting for me with a puzzled, lost expression in his eyes. I paced the floor and watched the clock with an increasing sense of worry and impatience.

It was ten o'clock before I was able to see the dentist. While I

27

sat in his chair it began to thunder and lightning. A high wind splattered rain against the windows. I thought I'd never seen the rain come down so hard. The dentist did extract one of my teeth, but I felt no pain. I was thinking of Henry the whole time, knowing how worried he must be. I was half-sick thinking of it.

By the time I got back to the ward it was close to noon. The Baron's bed was empty and his chair was gone. I expected to find him in the dayroom, but he wasn't there. I checked all of the sleeping rooms along the hall, then went down to the cafeteria, stopped to look in the visitor's room and the recreation room. Two orderlies were playing ping pong, but no one else was there. I stepped outside. The rain had stopped and my heart jumped to see two deep wheel marks in the muddy ground by the front steps. It looked as if the Baron had shot his chair out the front door, cleared the steps, and landed violently on the rutted ground. I followed the wheel marks across the yard until they stopped at the driveway. The sky was beginning to clear and there was the sound of dripping by the buildings and the trees, and water rushing down the gutters by the road. The air was wonderfully fresh, as if it had been washed completely clean, and a strong wind blew with a surprising force. As I started down the hard top path we'd often taken, I was trying to imagine in what spirit Henry had set out on his own. Whether he was perturbed or calm, and whether he'd gone looking for me, which seemed likely. I walked at a fast pace, but the Baron had gotten a good start on me. It was a half hour before I saw him on the path about a quarter mile ahead of me, moving along in an unhurried way. I felt delighted as a child to see him. I called his name, but the wind was blowing in my face. It swallowed up my voice. The Baron couldn't hear me, but I could see where he was going. He was almost at the point where the path drops sharply into a long sloping hill. At the bottom of this hill was the turn off for the dirt path up to our cliff view. I walked faster and began to shout at him, but the Baron never slowed or turned in my direction. In fact to my dismay he picked up speed. There was a sudden urgency to the way he spun his wheels, and I saw the chair leap forward. As he started down the hill, he was racing.

I was sure that he'd injure himself, and I began to run, still shouting to him. His head was bent so low that I could hardly see it, and he flew down the hill at a velocity that looked suicidal. I ran with all of my strength behind him and was relieved to see him make it safely to the bottom. "Henry, WAIT," I called to him, but he pressed ahead as hard as ever. He crossed the grass at a good clip and started up the high dirt path churning his wheels. The wind veered around and blew behind me then. It seemed to push my back with great harsh shoves. I doubled my speed and by the time the Baron had begun to falter halfway up the hill, I'd caught up with him, grabbed the chair, and pushed it with one long extended lunge up to the top and across the open patch of grass. My legs felt watery and strangely weak and I collapsed on the wooden bench with a feeling of exhaustion so acute, I thought I might be sick. The Baron was just as winded. We sat heaving and gasping, unable to speak. Our mountain view was buried in dense fog. It was impossible to see the valley. My lungs hurt me and I felt pain in my shoulders, gripping my neck and rising to my head where the blood was beating in my ears. The wind was even stronger on the cliff. It came at us in little blasts. The Baron's face was still bent forward. There was something dejected about the way his back remained curved over and his hands stayed holding the arms of his chair.

"Why did you run away from me?" I asked at last. Henry didn't look at me or move.

"I'm sorry about this morning," I said. "They sent me to the doctor and the dentist very early. You were asleep. I didn't want to wake you." Henry raised his head. His eyes were red. The misery in them was so intense, it shocked me. He didn't look at me. He stared out over the foggy trough of nothingness below and I could see that under his sadness was a layer of coldness and unforgiving distance he had made between us.

"There are some things I have to tell you. I should have told you long ago," I said. But the Baron remained stony and his aloofness made my words sound strangely foolish. I could almost sense that he was growing more distant from me by the minute, as if he were running physically away from me again and I'd begun to chase him. A gust of wind blew in my face. It whipped my hair and tugged at the strip of loosened bandage by the Baron's ear. I felt light-headed and wreckless. I thought I heard somebody whisper "Watch it, Paul. Just watch it." But the voice was pitiful and faint. The wind was stronger, lashing in my ears. It was blowing in my brain and all my thoughts were stirring, flying up and swirling in great arcs until my mind was spinning with them. I put my hands up to my face to stop the dizziness, the pressure and the knocking like great fists inside my head. I reached for the Baron's arm. I held onto it and I let my head fall down until it touched his sleeve. I began to speak to him. I was crying, and the voice I used was alien to me. It was a terrible voice, hoarse and low, which seemed to rise from some deep suffocating chasm and had to wrench and choke itself in order to escape. Yet once the voice had started, on and on it went like a machine switched on and driven separately from me. The words poured out with such a force, I felt I couldn't stop them if I tried. Words jumped out. Like things alive they leapt over each other in an effort for release. As they came, I heard the sound of drums begin, the noise of hurried marching feet, and a loud trumpet blast that sounded desperate, like a scream. Still my strange voice went on with the momentum of a river, and I told myself that if the army tried to overcome me, I would hurl myself over the cliff and wipe out the entire company in one grand explosion. Perhaps the General sensed the utter seriousness of my intention. The trumpet died away with a pathetic sigh, the drums and marching feet grew more remote and faint until I heard only the sound of my own stricken voice, this time more clearly. The grief was terrible in that weeping voice, so terrible that there was nothing I could do but listen with a sense of growing recognition. I listened and I saw a little white-washed farm house with two broken windows like two eyes, the door a gaping mouth wide open to the night. The house, set back from a dirt road, was vivid white under the moon which also bathed the wide surrounding fields and all the trees along the road in ghostly light. There was a soldier hurrying up the road with a carbine rifle tightly clutched against his chest. He was whimpering to himself and moaning, his darting eyes alarmed and wide with fear. The smells of the Italian countryside were an assault of sweetness to his nose, and the beauty of the night was something incomprehensible and appalling to the soldier, mad and AWOL, running from his men who even now were searching for him down the road. He stopped before the small abandoned house, the dismal face whose window eyes looked balefully at him while he stared back with every nerve alert, the moonlight pouring down, the rifle tightly pressed in two white hands that shook and trembled with a constant agitation. There was an unexpected noise within the house, a shuffling in the dark. The startled soldier sprang into a crouch, his rifle swung out from his chest, and when he saw a flash of white go by the door, he shot. He kept on shooting even when he heard a woman's scream and didn't stop until his gun was empty. The company commander, Captain Barker, was running up the road. And there were others, one who took away his gun, and one who ran up with a light and shone it on the dark-haired woman on the floor, thin and young, her white dress spattered with her blood, a child, a boy no more than nine, still clinging to her side, his body twitching, dying there before them. Captain Barker with a white ferocious face was saying "Christ, man, CHRIST look what you've done."

From a far distance I could feel the Baron's hand. It rested like protection on my head while my own ragged voice went on. It was the voice of an exhausted child, monotonous and flat, a voice that was familiar to me now.

VI.

Did I dream it that the rain began to pour while Henry and I were still up on the cliff? I could remember so well the feeling of icy rain soaking my back and how it fell like walls around us. I quickly pushed the Baron down the hill. The ground was slippery and muddy. The rain was blinding and I almost fell. Henry pointed to the chapel and we hurried into it for shelter. Once inside, the Baron wheeled himself right up the aisle. He pointed with excitement to the little organ by the altar, one that

I'd never noticed before. He wanted to examine it more closely. I pushed him up the step and had to lift him to the organ bench. I was surprised to see how excited he was and pleased to see his old exuberance. When he pressed a G and heard the sound of it, he clapped his hands. He gestured to the little pew behind the organ, and I sat there. Then, to my amazement, he began to play. Not haltingly or poorly as you would expect of a man with a damaged brain who'd never indicated that he knew an instrument. He played that organ easily and brilliantly—while I sat there levitated and transfixed. It seemed to me that I had never heard Bach played so well or Messaien or Dupré. He played piece after piece. I told myself perhaps the beauty of the music was so overwhelming because I hadn't heard real music since the war, only the canned sound they play over the speakers on the wards. I told myself that I had lost the critical ability to judge the quality of his playing. But the Baron had started a Bach toccata, one that I knew well, and I felt the power of that piece played to its fullest glory, so it was the genius of the music that came through the self-effacing ease and the excellence of Henry's playing. The rain had stopped and a ray of sun fell from the sacristy on Henry, shone on his greying head, flashed on his hands, and caught the dust that sparkled rising from the keys. He was playing flawlessly, and it was at that moment with a sense of creeping horror that I felt the hairs stand up on my neck. My eyes fell on the pumping feet and the helpless legs which leapt and danced over the pedals, and I had a sudden dead white feeling of pure fear that Henry Baron wasn't real.

I woke up in a strange room. The sun was shining in my eyes. There was an old man asleep in the bed next to me. He had two tubes in his nose and his arm was hooked up to an i.v. I was looking at him when my mother appeared beside my bed. Bill was standing behind her. She kissed my cheek and I smiled at her. "Don't try to speak, dear," she said, putting her hand over my mouth. "You've been very sick. The doctor wants you to rest and sleep as much as possible. Bill and I will be right here. Kathleen is coming too. You must try to sleep now."

I closed my eyes. I dreamed I was back on the ward in Henry's room. Two nurses were about to change his bandages. I was anxious to leave the room, but the Baron indicated urgently that he wanted me to stay. I stood at the end of his bed while the nurses removed the bandages strip by strip, starting at the forhead. Henry kept his eyes on me, and I was anxious not to show the slightest shock at anything revealed. His cheek bones were uncovered and I saw his nose. It was long and straight, without a sign of injury, an elegant, aristocratic nose. It was exactly the nose I would have expected the Baron to have. And yet when I saw the lower half of my friend's face, I gasped. Where was the sunken hollow of the cheek, the sheared-off chin, and the misshapen profile I'd so often seen? When the final swatch of bandage was removed, the face revealed was totally unmarred. I was reminded of Abe Lincoln when I saw the solemn dignity and the ugly beauty of the Baron's face. I stared at him and shook my head uncomprehendingly. "But why the bandages?" I asked. The Baron only smiled. This amazing man. He smiled.

When I woke up, I was smiling too. The room was dark and the old man was snoring loudly in the bed beside me. I kept thinking of Henry. I was remembering the way he'd played the organ in the chapel. Surely I must have dreamed it and the Baron must be real, I told myself, but I was afraid. Why was Henry's face still bandaged more than thirty years after the war? It seemed preposterous that I had never questioned it before. And why was it that in all the five months I had known him I could not remember any orderly or nurse ever referring to him or once saying the name of Henry Baron? Perhaps the army had made the Baron up just so that they could take him away from me. I suffered with my thoughts and never slept the rest of that night. In the morning I was still awake when Mrs. Cooley walked into the room.

"I was on my way to work," she said cheerfully. "I'd have come to visit you sooner, but I've been on vacation." She came over to the bed. I watched her, holding my breath, hoping she might mention Henry. She looked at me, and her face became concerned. "Poor Paul. Have you been feeling awfully lonely?" She reached into her purse and dabbed my eyes and my face with a Kleenex. I strained to speak, but Mrs. Cooley gripped my shoulder. "Don't, Paul. You mustn't talk," she said. She looked alarmed. "Haven't they told you?" she said. "You've had a stroke. You'll be fine, but you can't speak yet. Your speech has been affected." I listened, stunned, while she went on to tell me about the therapy they'd be starting. I felt strangely like laughing, the bitter laugh that comes after despair, when the mind is worn out with pain and turns away from it with irony and cold amusement, when the chain of human moods begins to roll again and life goes on and on and on.

The old man was gone from the bed beside me. I could hear my mother's voice out in the hall, talking to someone. The room was frightfully hot. A red-haired nurse came in and shut the window. "We're putting the air-conditioner on," she said. "You'll feel the difference soon." From where I lay the only view was one waving tree branch rising halfway up the window. The branch was heavy with dark leaves which were fully open and fully grown. I could see that it was a maple tree, and that it was well into summer. Time for my madness. Perhaps I was at this very moment mad, I thought. But then it came to me that there was no army, no sign of the army. The army was gone.

Wealth

ESTHER'S FAMILY WAS WEALTHY. Her father, mother, and especially her grandmother would have spoiled her if she'd ever let them. While she was small her grandmother Sutton liked to take her to F.A.O. Schwartz each birthday, and the store became a battleground between them. "Now you choose whatever you'd like, dear," the grandmother said, loud enough to turn heads, and she waved an arm so that all of her rings flashed in the light. Esther faced the whirring room of toys each year. The flutey whistle of a tiny train enchanted the air. She turned to meet the staring eyes of fifteen lavish dolls, breathed in the rising odor of temptation, and set her jaw. "But I don't want *anything*, Grammy," she said.

There was a dollhouse which was a mansion really. White columns at the porch, the door bell really rang. And when you turned a switch a little lamp came on in every room. Grandmother Sutton, wrapped in grey fur and smelling of lavender, pressed the girl as subtly as she could. "It would make *me* so happy if you'd have it, dear," she said. But Esther chose a little bear small enough to ride home in her pocket, and when they left the store, she was relieved.

What did she want? "Nothing," Esther always answered at birthdays, Christmas, or when anybody asked. The answer was a reflex which became a family joke, though it haunted the mother, Harriet, whose life was fueled by strong desires. Harriet dreamed of trips, of pretty dresses, shoes, of carpets, cars, of parties, of the million little wishes that never failed to pave her future with excitement. She longed to shower her three daughters with things she'd never had all the struggling years before her marriage. She had a love of comfort, would have liked it to be summer in New

England all year round. The winter strain of illness and cold had to be borne, but summer was meant to be delicious in her house. From the fresh squeezed orange juice at breakfast to the last embrace at night, the naps, the meals, the swimming, the quiet and the social life all were balanced to keep the Suttons so soothed and stimulated that every conscious moment ought to be a pleasure.

For as long as Esther lived at home the summer schedule never changed. Her mother's dream unravelled every morning. Harriet woke the children with a kiss at eight, stood at the open windows breathing in the view. "What a heavenly day its going to be," she'd say just as if she'd never said it before—so enthusiastic that her pale and languid children turned their faces to the wall away from the bright windows as if they had been robbed.

Six bedrooms were aired and tidied every morning. From nine to eleven the maid, Azelia, vacuumed, dusted, mopped and polished, changed the linen, rubbed the door brass till it shone. While they were small, the children were sent out on sunny days right after breakfast. Three quiet girls who played in the shady court or the garden close by the house where the noise poured out the open kitchen door, the clashing pots and banging cupboards and the mixer rising in a shriek above the vacuum. The cook, Delores, chattered with their mother, who liked to pick and arrange the flowers for the dining room herself. In the sunny garden the children played where the morning air danced and sparkled, a teeming sea of shining particles. There were yellow jackets, bees, dragon flies, and darting birds which crowded the apple tree until it was a living pulse of cries. The laughter of the women drifted out to touch the children like a drug—a drug of contentment so intense that Esther often rose from the depths of an imaginary game like a swimmer desperate for air, as if she had been fooled or caught off guard by all the humming business of the morning. It was the same some nights when her mother rocked her just at dusk by the window where the summer sky was fading violet and the smell of honeysuckle was so strong. Her mother's lovely voice and cheek upon her cheek inveigled her to sleep with lullabies. But then some nights a larger consciousness awakened. The sweet air was heavy and her mother's voice became a weight pressing her down until she struggled to sit up. Fear was in the room, magnetic to such comfort, lurking in every shadow like the underworld of truth that lived behind her mother's wall of cheerfulness.

The morning hours passed so quickly. The groceries arrived. The gardener carried up the mail. By eleven Harriet had made her phone calls, was writing letters to her friends in Tulsa or New York, ones she'd met on trips to Greece or France or ones she planned to meet. By eleven the kitchen noise was muted, transformed to rising odors. Apple pie for Doctor Sutton who would drive the two miles from his office to take his mid-day meal at home.

The children were put down to nap right after lunch, though Esther could never sleep on those eternal afternoons. The silence was oppressive. It was so quiet she could hear the slightest breeze high in the elm leaves, the filter humming by the pool. The drone of a far off lawn mower was the only hint of human life, or her mother's sigh which rose up two stories as she turned her body in the sun or poured lemonade from a sweating silver pitcher so the sound of the ice hitting her glass was like a pistol shot.

At five o'clock the family showered off the day, appearing fresh for evening. Harriet, darkly tanned, a striking blonde in a flow-ered dress, wore gold earrings, trailed cologne. The father, im-maculate and tall, wore a jacket of seersucker or linen. The scent of lime was on his smooth cheek. For supper there was chilled salmon with green sauce. There were fresh peas, a garden salad, homemade bread.

"Delicious," everyone said. Across from Esther sat her sisters, Lindsay and Elaine, their faces pinkly scrubbed, with matching ribbons in their hair. The sisters smiled across the table at each other, their hearts as spotless as their dresses. Their senses were so lulled by food, by summer life in the spacious, breezy house, they hardly ever fought.

"I think we are the luckiest people in the world," their mother sighed. Then Delores cleared the table. The parents had their coffee on the porch just off the dining room. "I'm so happy,

37

Ben," they heard their mother say. "You've given me everything, you know."

"Darling," their father whispered. Esther could see the light flood into his face as he spoke the word, then touched Harriet's hand or stretched across to kiss her cheek. He always looked so tired, half dead some days, his face completely white. Why did their mother hound him to go out so many nights, appear at the door where he'd fallen asleep too tired even to read the paper. But there she was, all flushed in the face, excited. "Why, Ben, did you forget the Newmans?" she'd say, surprised. "We're supposed to be there in twenty minutes."

"Do you like my dress?" she'd ask, looking so pleased that he couldn't resist her any more than he could a patient in the middle of the night or Lindsay and Elaine when they crawled into his lap to kiss his sleeping face—just as thoughtless and selfish as Harriet. He never complained. He was so good, so good that whenever Esther thought of him she felt a pain right over her heart—the same as when she'd see him standing by the bird bath or the pool, stiff and formal as a stranger taking in the view—as if the property belonged entirely to Harriet, the gardener and the cook, and he were just a lonely guest who had no real home anywhere at all.

Even Grandma Sutton noticed his fatigue. When she came to visit twice a year there was tension in the house, all through the pretty rooms where angry words were seldom heard. Harriet would do anything to avoid the slightest tiff, but the grandmother always said exactly what she thought.

"He's exhausted, Hattie," she'd say, and her eyes had all the flash and hardness of two diamonds. "The social life you keep is going to kill him."

"You're so wrong, dear," their mother blithely cried, tossing her curly head. "He needs the change of pace. He says so himself —that it relaxes him to be with people he likes."

"Why, Harriet, he knows it's what *you* want," the grandmother said, exasperated. The children were awed to hear the truth so simply stated.

Esther was nine before she dared to break the family rhythm.

38

She set her clock for three and lay in the dark, enthralled, as if that abandoned hour were an island protected by emptiness stillness. In the morning she rose earlier than the rest. She came to dinner late without a shower, declining family outings, begging off from church.

"I'd rather not go out tonight," she said just like a grown up.

"But what will you *do* all evening?" Harriet cried, dismayed. Lindsay was going away to school in the fall. Another year and Elaine would be leaving too. After that who could say when they'd ever be together.

"But we'll be together in the summers." Esther argued, stubborn as always and so unlike her sisters who followed their mother eagerly through the flowery smelling stores she loved on wondrous shopping sprees. Already they spoke of Peugeots and Aston-Martins, of clothes and shoes and trips abroad.

"It isn't normal for a child not to want things," Harriet repeated to the father.

"But she doesn't seem to be unhappy," he replied. "Anyway, you can't expect everyone to have as many appetites as you do, darling," he said with admiration, and he kissed her upturned pretty mouth.

Watching the family drive off for the evening, Esther felt triumphant. She heard Delores humming in the kitchen, thought she'd visit with her. But first she dropped into her father's chair, sat surveying the long living room. Her mother's cigarette was still smoking in the ash tray on the coffee table, but already the room was transformed. The pink chair by the fireplace was twice as pretty. The more she stared at it, the more its color deepened like a blush. It arched its lovely back so far—as if it ached to move—and would have if she hadn't turned her eyes away in time. The newly covered flowered couch was gay and frivolous, held in check by the onyx lamp which shed a scathing light upon it. Only the old blue rug behind the couch with the stain her mother tried to hide was always the same whether the family was there or not. It seemed to be comfortable on its back, gazing up amused at the flighty furniture and the snobby Steuben candy dish. The tall glass lamp with the cream silk shade was as elegant and showy as her Grandmother Sutton. "All of your girls are pretty, Hattie," she'd said on her last visit. "But Esther's going to be the beauty." Grandma Sutton had been a beauty once herself. You could see this even in the morning when she took her tea in bed. Her hair was neatly brushed, brown hair without a sign of grey. She had a silvery, flawless skin and eyes of palest blue. She wore a set of pearls that matched her white lace jacket—a bracelet and a set of diamond rings. She didn't kiss the children, but pressed her cheek to theirs. Her cheek was cool, even in summer, and fragrant, softer than any other cheek. "I want you to have this," she'd said to Esther on her last visit. Around the girl's neck she clasped a tiny gold chain. "It was mine when I was a girl, and I want you to have it," she said as if she wouldn't take an argument.

Touching her neck, Esther was surprised to find the necklace was still there. She rose from her father's chair, then seemed to float across the room to the mirror by the door. Even the air was living, almost electric in every hollow room of the house whenever the family was gone. She could move so freely through this air. She could run to the top of the stairs and back in half the time it usually took. At the mirror the room looked stark in its reflection. She could feel the sharpening personalities of tables, chairs, lamps, and paintings in a rising glow behind her. The room and the air were frightfully alive and she was a real girl, so real she could see the solid shape her body carved in space. She held her braids against her head, stared into the staring eyes, at the dark hair above the pale face, the serious little mouth, and the chain of shining gold at her neck. She turned the chain until she found the clasp, then dropped the necklace into the empty candy dish, and floated down the hall to see Delores.

Delores also was changed whenever Harriet was away. She'd sit in the scoured kitchen at the table, resting her long face on one reddened palm while she drank her coffee, and she'd talk to the children as equals in a confidential voice as if there wasn't anything she wouldn't tell them. They knew about her husband Eddie, who drank a bottle of whiskey every day and how the night before she left him for good he beat her up so badly that he knocked out her front tooth. "Can we see the tooth?" the children

40

often asked. Then Delores would remove the discolored tooth to show them it was false. She'd hold it up like a relic and stare at it with interest. "Think twice before you marry, girls," she'd say. Delores was full of stories, stories of death and suffering and illness, but only when their mother was away.

The sound of the car on the drive was an alert. Before Harriet reached the front door—while her footsteps were still clicking up the walk, the house was ready for her—back to normal. The hollow rooms upstairs were filled and warmed to greet her. In the living room the light was muted gold, as soft as firelight, and the entire house was harmless, a cherished showplace sitting on a hill above the town, a yellow dream that people stopped to stare at, men and women who paused in idling cars beyond the gate or children and parents who left their cars to stand sometimes in a row all gripping the bars of the high iron fence like prisoners to catch a better view. Esther was the girl in the starchy pinafore high upon the hill, caught in the middle of the garden walk with flowers rising all around her—tulips, hyacinths, and lilacs all frozen in the perfect picture till the watching people sighed and turned away to leave.

The Sutton sisters said they longed to travel. They dreamed of Africa and China, Italy and Spain. Not one of them had ever spent a night away from home. Without directly saying so, their mother had discouraged it. She picked them up from school in the yellow station wagon which matched the color of the house, and she seemed to whisk them home as quickly as she could.

"Hello, Mrs. Sutton," the teachers called, in special, lilting voices. Their eyes reached all the way across the street to touch the new fur hat, the black kid gloves upon the steering wheel, the perfect profile turning mildly toward them with a smile as self-possessed and distant as all their dreams of wealth had led them to expect.

"Run up and wash your hands and faces," Harriet said as soon as they reached the house, as if there were something tainted or tacky about the school and all the milling children. Taking her cue, the sisters made few friends. In the school yard they sat sedately on the benches or the swings, as if immune to the entire mob of racing, shouting children. Lindsay and Elaine were in-separable. Esther was happy to entertain herself. At home she ran the length of the lawn in the company of a hundred laughing children, all shrieking and colliding, their dream faces turned sweetly toward her, appearing and disappearing, happy as saints to do her bidding.

Afternoons at home the sisters filled the empty hours until dinner. While they played, they felt Harriet's presence like the sun at the windows and the doors shining down approval on their quiet games. They were pleased to please their mother, as if her happiness were frail and crucial. The thought of disappointing her was painful to them. She didn't like to talk about her past, the time before her marriage, but sometimes she'd hold up one of their dolls or open a closet to admire a row of their dresses with hurt and pleasure in her face. "You girls have everything I ever dreamed of as a child," she'd say, reminding them with surprise that once she'd led another life.

In dreams, long nightmares, Esther saw her mother cry as if her heart would break—saw her flung across her bed and sobbing in the dark, her hair disheveled and her face distorted in a way that was so alien and terrifying, the girl woke up screaming. She had the dream repeatedly the summer she turned twelve. Each time it was so real, she went to her mother's bed to see if it were true.

"Poor darling," Harriet whispered. "I'm not crying. See?"

"I wonder why you have this funny dream," she'd say, awake and smiling with an arm about the child as she walked her to her room.

"Shall I stay with you a while?" she asked—then climbed into the small bed, curled around the shivering girl.

"Are you sure you aren't crying, Mother?" Esther kept repeating in the dark.

"Of course not, dear. How often do you ever see me cry?"

Esther could remember only twice seeing her mother in tears. "Forgive me," Harriet had said, embarrassed to be crying, as if unhappiness were a weakness and long extended grief amounted to a sin. She couldn't endure the sight of herself in tears. The day that Lindsay left for prep school, she had wept. The girl wore a pink tweed suit and high heeled shoes. Her fly-away blonde hair was neatly braided, pinned up high above gold earrings. Lindsay ruffled Esther's hair and kissed her cheek although they never had been close. The scent of her cologne was new. Standing by the car beside a heap of luggage, she looked already severed from the family, as if she were a finished product they could finally judge. Only Lindsay's eyes, which were red from crying, were part of the past.

It was the same the following year when their father drove off with Elaine. Harriet spent the morning in her room and Esther stood in the hall outside the bedroom door, afraid to see her mother, who cried so forcefully, as if each child were being driven off to death or torture and she were able to foresee misery, so much ugliness, indignity and turmoil, and the way each child would have to suffer, pay for all the years of sweetness, for so many perfect days and fearless nights, and all the beauty she had tried to give them.

Lindsay and Elaine were miserable away at school. They cried themselves to sleep at night and couldn't wait for their vacations. Now that they were gone, Esther felt her mother draw her closer. Often they napped together, climbing the dark staircase after lunch through layers of cooling air up to Harriet's spacious room where the shades were already drawn and blowing out over the open windows. It was early June. Mother and daughter kicked off their sandals, slipped out of their dresses.

"Delores will call us in an hour," Harriet said with satisfaction. In their slips they lay beside each other on the heavy, white spread, so heavy it was cooler than the pillows into which they pressed their warm faces.

"This is heaven," sighed the mother, who'd been up since seven so the morning had been long and wonderfully busy. She patted Esther on the cheek. "Have you ever thought how lucky it is we've had this time to get so close?" she said. They'd gone out shopping almost every weekend, gone to hairdressers, stopped at scores of little tea rooms for their lunches.

43

"Essie and I—we've had the loveliest time together, Ben," she'd heard her mother say. "I want you to see the things we've bought," she'd said, ignoring his fatigue, taking him to the guest room, which was draped with purchases—dresses, skirts and coats, boots and shoes and luggage. Esther imagined her father feigning interest and surprise as Harriet opened bags and boxes, held up brightly colored sweaters which he didn't even see. The helpless way he looked, perpetually drawn to her excitement as if it were a flame whose light reflected in his face.

"Of course she didn't want any of this," Harriet had said with a little laugh. "But she went along with all of it just to please me. Wasn't that dear?"

Now lying beside her mother on the bed, Esther looked at Harriet's sleeping face. Asleep, she looked so young. It was hard to believe that she ever had been poor, deprived of anything.

Shadows of waving branches danced upon the shades. The birds and chattering squirrels made such a noise just beyond the windows where the hottest sun of the day beat on the shades as if it would do anything to break into the room. Harriet slept and Esther lay awake and restless, though she kept her body still. She closed her eyes but couldn't sleep. It was as if a light within her brain would not go out, but burned with a steady brightness down upon a blinding inner view, a vast expanse of emptiness and stillness which stretched in all directions to the sky. There was only air, mirror-still and sharply clear, odorless and sound-less, through which she gazed without distraction or temptation, her face suffused with longing and desire.

A Certain View

Delia

DAVEY WORE A WINTER JACKET in summer and he didn't feel the heat. His mother, Delia, said he shivered and he cried unless he had the coat, so she let him wear it in spite of what the doctors and the neighbors and his father said. They told her she was just as touched as the boy. But she let him wear the coat and she allowed him to sit on the front porch from one to three o'clock each afternoon, which was all that he wanted. He wouldn't speak much. Some weeks he went for days not saying a word. The doctors said this was a bad sign. But he could still tell time, which excited Delia and kept her hope alive. If she held him in the house past one o'clock, he cried as if his heart would break. But as soon as he was settled in his heavy jacket on the porch, he was serene. He even smiled, Delia said, and it was this smile that guided her, not the advice of any doctor, neighbor, or wife-abandoning husband who hadn't seen his son in six months and now was calling every day or showing up with roses or chocolate covered cherries by the box.

The sun beat down directly on them those two hours on the porch. The sweat poured off Davey till his clothes were soaked. Delia sat beside him, served and made him drink a pitcher of lemonade in an afternoon. She also made him wear a straw hat and dark glasses, though he didn't want to. Sometimes he'd tear off the hat and toss it over the porch railing fifteen times in an afternoon. And she'd have to retrieve the hat each time or the glasses which he also threw away. She was afraid he'd get sun stroke without the hat or go blind if he didn't wear the glasses. After his accident, Davey was fascinated by the sun. Delia said he would have stared at it all afternon if she'd let him. He turned eight that summer and she had to watch him as closely as a two year old.

Afternoons when the mercury hit ninety-eight degrees and there wasn't a breath of moving air on Cherry Street, Delia's long face was crimson. She kept a dab of cream on the end of her nose. Sometimes she read to him for hours, though he gave no sign that he understood it or enjoyed it. But he'd used to love it when she read aloud to him, and he'd used to love her corn muffins, her home canned stewed tomatoes, and her rhubarb pies. So now she cooked them often, though his appetite was not the same and he never spoke of food. She said she felt as if she had to woo him back, convince him it was worth it to be well.

The father, Lester, showed up daily at his lunch hour. His tires squealed as he made the turn from Brighton Avenue, always in a hurry. He'd swing his car right up to the curb, lurch it to a stop, then trot up the walk carrying flowers, candy, or whatever else he imagined was the price of admission. When he saw Delia and Davey sitting on the porch, he always looked surprised. The spectacle of the winter jacket, the dark glasses, the straw hat, and Delia's red face enraged him every time.

"You'll kill that kid!" he shouted. But Delia didn't answer him no matter how he ranted. She wasn't even angry with him any more, this man with liquor on his breath who'd never cried in all the time that they were married. Now, whenever he called or came to the house, he'd break down.

Mary Taggard

Some people's lives are so ordinary that even the suffering, the deaths, and all the difficulties they ever know seem ordinary too; just what you might expect in the normal course of a life. My family was like this. My father was a steady working man, not specially liked or disliked in town. My mother was the same. She was happy to have her house, her husband and her children. She wanted nothing more. Not anyone in my family was specially smart or specially good looking. I was just as plain as all the rest. The only difference was, I couldn't accept it. I never was satisfied with myself, not with my looks or my hand-me-down clothes or the way I didn't shine in school or anything. Most often I kept my feelings to myself, feelings of shame and disappointment. Just once I remember I cried. One day in the kitchen with Mother. I was about thirteen at the time. What surprised me was that she cried with me. She sat there in her worn house dress and her raggedy slippers, she put her sewing down, and she cried as if she understood exactly how useless and how dull I felt.

There was a teacher I once had, Miss Potter in fifth grade. I've never forgotten her. She took me aside one day and she said, "There's nothing wrong with your mind, Mary Taggard. You could be making all A's if you wanted to. You just don't try."

"Oh, I *do* try," I insisted. But old Miss Potter shook her head and smiled as if she knew something I didn't know.

Mother always said I was the most affectionate of her children, always wanting to be kissed or held. When Father would come home at night, I'd climb into his lap and sit there curled against him while he read his paper.

"I love you, Papa," I would say, and I'd feel a weight be lifted off my chest when I said the words.

When I was small I had a rag doll named Marie, and for about three years I carried that doll everywhere with me till it got so beat up Mother was ashamed to let me take it out in public. But no one had the heart to separate me from Marie. I must have kissed those button eyes a million times and the red stitched mouth, and even when I was older, I couldn't throw that doll away. I packed her carefully in a shoe box up in the attic, and she's still there today.

When I was a girl, I used to go to the movies all the time, and I'd wish so hard that I could fall in love. Even if the man didn't love me back, I'd wish that I could know what it was like to love someone that way. When I was in my teens some nights I'd feel so full of love, I'd think it was a living thing already there inside me even though I had no one to give it to.

But I never did find any man I could admire so much, or one who ever wanted me either, which is the disappointment of my life.

There was one boy named Bob Dover who liked me once. He lives in Ray County now with a wife and three kids. Our last year in high school he kept calling me on the phone and asking me out. "Heaven sakes, why don't you go out with the poor boy?" Mother said. Finally one night I did. He took me to a movie and we stopped at Kaylees for a bite to eat. I was a shy girl and nervous, but we laughed a good deal. I think we laughed the whole of that evening till he brought me home. Then he stopped the car and he looked at me with such a serious face. "You know I've always liked you a lot, Mary," he said. I was so dumbfounded that I couldn't think of a way to answer him. I just froze up inside and couldn't move or speak. I don't know how long we sat there. At last he walked me up to the house and he left without a word. Even today, I think of the serious look on his face, how hard it was for him to say those words, and the awful silence afterwards. He never called me again. Maybe he felt foolish. After that, no one ever asked me out. Bob Dover was the only one.

As far back as I can remember there were always people I envied. People who were handsome or beautiful or smart, who had a lot of poise and dignity and confidence, the ones that reminded me of my own weak points. Delia King was one of those people. She moved into the house across the street from us the summer I turned thirty. Father was dead. He'd just keeled over on the front lawn the year before and died of a heart attack before he even got to the hospital. Mother hadn't been well ever since. My sister and brother were both married and moved away with homes and children of their own, so it was only natural that I was the one expected to care for Mother. Not that I didn't want to. Mother and I were always close. We got on well. But that year was hard. My job at Federal Savings, where I'd worked for twelve years, got on my nerves. The routine of it. Everything got on my nerves that year, it seemed. Even the house upset me. I never could keep it as clean as I wanted to and everywhere I looked needed paint or fixing. Mother told me not to let it bother me so much. She said we'd hire Dickie Berry or one of the other high school boys to do some of the work, which was the only way we could afford it. With the small pension Mother had from Father and my salary, we didn't have a lot to spare.

Delia and her husband Lester took the old Ashburton place across the street. Their boy, Davey, was only six the summer they moved in. Lester King owned the largest sporting goods store in the county. It was called KINGS SPORTS and it was said to be a thriving business. Delia was a school teacher. When she first introduced herself to Mother one day while I was at work, she said she'd be starting to teach at the grammar school in the fall. She hoped she'd be able to get the house done over before she started work.

The Ashburton house is the oldest on our street. It had been empty for about eight years, ever since Ann Ashburton passed away. Paint was peeling everywhere and there probably wasn't one room that didn't need paint or fixing. It was a little Victorian-style house up on a hill with a nice front porch all decorated with gingerbread. You knew it could be a sweet looking place if someone did it over right. Delia hired a whole crew of carpenters and painters, and all summer long she worked right with them. Every day when I'd come home at five, I'd see some new improvement. She chose the nicest shade of yellow for the house. The shutters and the front door were painted black, and the iron fence that runs along the street. Delia put up new hedges all around the porch and a dogwood and a little crab apple on the front lawn. She ripped up the old stone walk and put down slate. By September the place was so pretty, it was hard to believe the difference. The brass knocker on the front door and all the windows gleamed like brand new. Mother took the Kings one of her famous crab meat pies, and one Saturday Delia invited us to see what she'd done to the inside. She showed us every room, and I thought to myself I'd never seen a lovelier little house, not in any magazine, not ever. We sat in the sunny kitchen sipping lemonade, admiring her new tile floor, the tall pine cabinets, the huge refrigerator, the shiny new stove, and it was all as gay and cheerful as Delia herself appeared to be. She was a tall, full-bodied woman, but she kept her figure trim. She was forty-two, she told us. She'd been married late and thanked her stars she'd still been young enough to have a child. "He's the treasure of my life," she said, pointing out the window at the tow-haired boy who was playing in the yard.

You wouldn't say that Delia King was pretty. Her face was long. Her mouth and nose were large, but her eyes were a startling blue of a deep color you don't often see. They stood out from her fair skin and they shone with energy. Her hair was dark and sleek and she wore it swept up neatly in a bun. When she sat across from us that morning, I thought how fresh, how clean she looked. Her left hand rested on the table with the sun showing up the wedding band and the diamond solitaire which sparkled blue in the light. I wondered how she kept her hands so smooth and white with all the gardening and house work. Her finger nails were perfect, nicely shaped and polished red to match the color of her mouth.

"I thought you might be sisters," Delia said. "You look so much alike." Mother and I smiled. Everyone always thought I was the image of her. We had the same brown hair, a mousy brown that wouldn't keep a set. We both wore glasses and we had the same long necks and freckled arms and bony hands. We even dressed alike and wore each other's clothes. I always imagined the picture we made when we walked down Main Street on a Saturday to shop—two bean poles, tall and thin as rails in slacks and sleeveless tops with long arms hanging down. My father always called my mother "Olive Oyl." Her clothes hung on her, and her shoes, like mine, were large, size ten. He'd bring home ice cream, honey donuts, or a chocolate cake, the kind she liked. Anything to make her put on weight. But she was a picky eater just like me. The more a person pressed her, the less she'd take.

"Such an attractive woman," Mother said on the way home from Delia's. I wondered if people always looked as neat or as decrepit as their houses. I thought of our dark kitchen with the sink full of dishes, the worn linoleum so full of grime you'd never get it clean, not if you scrubbed it on your hands and knees for a whole week. I wondered why it never bothered Mother. She didn't seem to have a trace of envy in her. She liked her house exactly as it was. After supper and the dishes, she'd sit on the same sofa where she'd sat most evenings but the rare exception for as far back as I could remember. With her slippered feet up on the faded hassock, her knitting or crocheting in her lap, and the light reflecting off her glasses, she'd look the same as when our father sat beside her and we children lay out on our stomachs in a row in front of television, as if there wasn't any place she'd rather be.

Some nights when I'd be restless, I'd look across at Mother with the lamp warming up her shoulder, lighting up the grey strands in her hair, and I'd see so much contentment in her face, the empty, peaceful look of someone who has no longings, no great hopes or shining expectations; someone who is totally accepting and resigned. I'd hear the hall clock ticking off the minutes in that steady way that got my nerves on edge, and I'd feel an anger rising up in me towards Mother, who never noticed time and had no fear of death. I'd wonder if she'd ever in her life thought highly of herself enough to feel afraid or angry or dissatisfied. She seemed surprised that she had ever married, borne three children, cooked, shopped, and kept a house, almost as if she'd never dreamed of anything for herself and had expected nothing. I'd think how wrong the people were who said we looked alike. For all of her thinness Mother always had a softness and a sweetness to her that I never had. It seemed to me the older I got, the harder and more bitter I appeared.

Delia

The doctors hadn't wanted her to take him home. Delia listened to them while she looked down at the white-faced child in the steely bed who stared up at the ceiling hardly blinking all day long. He'd hemorrhaged in his brain, they said. They couldn't tell how bad the damage was. It would be months before they'd know.

"I never should have let him go. He was too young to be out

at night," she kept repeating. The doctors turned away from the blue, imploring eyes. She could just see Davey and Fred Pease walking home together from the movies. How they stopped beside the school and climbed the fire ladder up to the roof of the gymnasium. Davey never saw the skylight in the dark. He was standing on it when the glass shattered and he fell sixty feet down to the gym floor. Delia took that fall a thousand times while she sat beside his bed. She felt her feet go through the glass and how the gleaming hardwood floor leapt up with such a vicious speed as if it had been coiled and waiting for a boy to fall.

The doctors wanted her to send him to another larger hospital fifty miles away from her for rehabilitation. "You've got to face it that he may not ever be the same," they said right in front of the child, as if they'd given up on him already. She argued with the doctors every day, who said she'd no idea how demanding it would be to have him home. Yet still she hesitated to insist, and she sat in the hospital like someone waiting for a signal. Then one afternoon Davey turned and looked right at her. He focussed on her face so clearly that her heart began to pound. "Mama," was all that he said and then he closed his eyes, but Delia thought her heart would burst. Right then, she said, she knew he would be well.

She took him home, and for the first few weeks Lester showed up like a nightmare in the middle of each day. Just when Delia had gotten the boy settled on the porch, and when the two of them were wrapped in the fierce heat and drinking up the silence of the street as if it were a cure. She'd hear the screech of Lester's car and then he would appear just like a stranger hurrying up the walk. Six months ago he'd left her for another woman, a girl he didn't even love named Dawn Sidelle, young enough to be his child. He no longer saw the girl and he lived alone on the other side of town. The rumor was that he'd become a heavy drinker and that he blamed himself for Davey's fall as much as if he'd pushed the boy with his own hands. He went around with a grim or gloomy face and if he ever saw a husband straying from his wife, he lectured him with all the fire of a preacher.

"You're going to kill that kid in all this heat," Lester would shout, but he always stayed below them on the lawn, afraid to set one foot up on the porch, as if the twenty pounds she'd gained in those six months had made her huge and terrifying to him. He'd thrust his face right up at her in the harsh light so she could see how much he'd changed. She couldn't help but notice how deep and crooked the lines were across his forehead. And his hair had thinned, lost all its shine. It was receding like a curtain slowly rising to reveal an ever larger view of misery and pain. Even the color of his skin was not the same. It never was that dusky, dirty color, stained like wine. And his cheek bones showed like death under the taut, leathery skin. She found it hard to look at him. Staring at the rumpled suit, at the glaring spot on his tie, she felt nothing at all.

"Think of the boy, Lester. It can't be good for him to see you so upset," she said. She always called him Lester now, Never Les or Lee the way she used to. "If you can't control yourself, I'd rather you didn't come here anymore," she said, but her voice was not unkind. He might have been one of her eighth grade students acting out of line.

"Here," he'd say, handing up the flowers or the candy. Then he'd stand there staring up at Davey or at her with stricken eyes, saying nothing. The longer he stayed, the more oppressed Delia felt. He was not the man she'd married and the boy who sat so deathly pale and silent like a statue in the sun was not her boy. Her Davey never could have sat so still to save his life.

Mary Taggard

I know it worried Mother to see how sad and broody I became after I turned thirty. I was like a different person, so nervous and so hard to please, like the fairy story of the Princess and the Pea. Nothing satisfied me. You'd have thought I wasn't even expecting to turn thirty, the way it took me by surprise. "Am I really that old?" I asked Mother, as if I had been dreaming all those years and just waked up in time to see that life was passing me by.

"Heavens, Mary. Thirty isn't old," Mother said. "You've got to eat more, honey. You're turning into skin and bones." But I could hardly touch food for the longest time and I couldn't sleep either. I'd be up and pacing the floor at least one night out of every three. I can't think of the number of times poor Mother showed up at my door at 3 a.m. with a cup of hot milk.

"Get into bed and drink this down. It'll help you sleep," she'd say, and we'd sit and look at each other like two ghosts, pale faced and hollow-eyed without our glasses in the dead of night when the silence was so thick it seemed we were the only living souls awake in Chilton. She'd make me finish every drop. Then she'd kiss me on the forehead. "Try to sleep now, Mary," was all she'd say, and I'd be grateful that she knew me well enough never to question me or pry into my thoughts. "Thank you, Mum," I'd say. But I'd never tell her what was bothering me. I'm sure it would have eased her mind no end if I'd been open with her, but I've always had a lot of pride, and it's a terrible thing. Almost as bad as envy.

It was all I could do to get myself to work those days. I hated that job for the longest while. I wanted to quit so many times, but I didn't let myself. When I'd get home, I'd be so tired out, I'd fall into the easy chair beside my bedroom window and I'd sit there like a person who's been dreaming and wants to see the hard realities of things. I had a million thoughts and most of them were sad. It was so easy to be sad. I'd think of marriage, how beautiful, like a miracle it seemed. The way at church you'd see a husband take his wife's arm without needing to explain or hold her waist as if his hand belonged there. The way you'd see a married couple out to supper in a restaurant or dancing, so at ease together that they didn't need to speak. I'd think how proud a man and wife must be when they'd go out in public, announcing to the world that they had found and chosen each other out of everyone.

I'd remember how the people at the bank used to tease me. "When are you going to get married, Mary? Who are you saving yourself for?" they'd say, and I'd always toss it off with some remark so they'd never know how much those questions made me cringe inside. I'd think of how nobody ever teased me about marriage anymore. Not since I'd turned thirty.

Delia

When she first met Lester, Delia thought she'd never seen a man with such a dark, despondent face. He hardly spoke at first, but his eyes reached out to her with such a power, they sometimes held her tight like arms across a table so she couldn't move. When she looked at him too long, she felt a lostness and a dizziness come over her, as if she could drown or disappear in those deep eyes which seemed to have no bottom and no end of sadness in them. She wondered how a man could ever have become so hopeless. When Lester talked about his childhood, he remembered beatings, fights, times when he was teased or slighted, scorned or shamed.

"*Something* good must have happened to you," Delia kept repeating, and Lester would smile at the urgent way she said this, a wide and wondrous smile that totally transformed his face. Whenever Delia saw this smile, she stared at him, transfixed. His eyes danced and he looked so young, like a different man, the one she wanted him to be.

"You're so beautiful," he'd say at moments when she least expected it, and he'd hold her tight and press her head so hard against his chest, she could feel the whole of his body trembling.

He seemed amazed that she would marry him. "Pinch me," he kept saying in the weeks before the wedding. "I know I must be dreaming. And on his face she saw continually the disbelieving smile that made her feel she had the power of the sun to warm and light every part of a vast darkness.

The morning of their wedding, he was radiant. When they came out of the church, the sun poured down out of a sky so solid blue, she thought she'd never seen the world so clear. The sun was bouncing off the houses and the cars, the bushes and the trees all blowing in the breeze, the lawn so magnified that she could count each spike of grass, as if her happiness had let her see all things exactly as she wanted them to be.

55

They took a small apartment, the top floor of a stucco building with a wide screen porch and a view of the whole valley and the river. Delia hung up plants and pictures and new flower printed curtains in the sunny rooms until they looked so gay, she sometimes had to stop and stare at them. Lester hardly noticed how pretty she had made the place. From the moment they were married, she saw a change in him, a look of worry always on his face.

"What is it, Les?" she'd ask him, but he wouldn't tell her. Sometimes he'd be so distant and pre-occupied, he wouldn't even answer. Often she'd wake at 5 a.m. and see the bed beside her empty. She'd search the rooms, but he'd be gone. He'd never mention where he went. One time she found him sitting on the porch with the summer morning laid out like a dream before him, the soft light flashing on the water, and all the birds were singing out as if their hearts were in their voices. His face was so forlorn, it shocked her.

"What is it, Les?" she cried. "Are you sorry that you married me?"

"For God's sake, Delia. Let me be," was all he said.

As if someone had cracked a whip, he took two extra jobs. He was a certified accountant, but he worked nights as a tax specialist and over weekends he showed houses for Marquesa Realty. She'd never known a man who worked so hard. He had no friends and never socialized or seemed to give himself the slightest bit of pleasure.

"I want you have the best," he said when she protested. "I want to give you everything someday."

"But I don't care about money," she cried. "I don't want a lot of things." The more she argued with him, the more grim and silent he would be. Sometimes the sight of his drawn face was like a weight that lay on her and crushed her. She'd feel a flash of fear and wonder if the marriage was a terrible mistake.

But then one night she'd wake to find him leaning over her, smoothing back her hair and whispering her name in a voice so strange and heavy with desire that all resistance flowed right out of her. Sometimes the sound of his voice alone could call up such an unknown part of her that never had been touched by anyone but him, making her moan or cry out before he even had begun to kiss her. He'd touch her slowly, bring each part of her to life, as if a light shone on her, and she felt so naked she would want to hide. But still he'd hold her and he wouldn't stop until she'd given herself up to him completely and her body moved as if it had a wild free mind all of its own and wasn't hers at all.

"My beauty," he would whisper in a voice as strange and ardent as the moonlight falling pale and sacred on their bed. His face was silver and exalted, and Delia felt so light, as if her body had no weight and floated up to him.

"My God, I love you," he would whisper, and Delia would feel that she was his and that she'd never been so loved.

"I'm not an easy man to live with," Lester said those nights when love words poured so easily from him. "It's not much of a marriage with me gone so much," he'd say out of the stillness, smoothing back her hair and looking down at her with eyes as dark and gentle as the air which blew across their bed. "It won't always be like this," he'd say. "But if I couldn't give you certain things, I couldn't stand myself." Delia would kiss his face and think how nothing mattered when she felt so close to him like this.

"I want you to be happy," she would tell him softly. "That's the only thing I want."

In the morning when he'd be so silent, even cool towards her, she'd find it hard to believe he was the same man who had showered her with praises in the dark and rocked her in his arms as if he'd never let her go. Sometimes he'd be so much a stranger when she sat across from him at breakfast, she'd be ashamed to think of things he'd said and done the night before.

Mary Taggard

Mrs. Flannery at the bank has a little sign that she keeps right at the front of her desk. "Smile. It Won't Hurt You," the sign says. She's kept it there for years, and it's always irritated me. The idea of smiling all the time for no good reason like a clown.

Whenever I notice that sign, I burn, but I also think of Delia King and how it gave you a lift just seeing her walking toward you on the street when she first moved to town. It wasn't just the pretty clothes or the friendly way she'd greet you. She always seemed so happy. More than anyone I knew. She gave the impression that she loved her life. After church you'd see the women flock around her, wanting her for luncheons, teas, or supper parties. Just wanting to be with her. She hadn't been in town a year before it seemed she'd always lived here. She sang in our church choir, was on the altar guild, the League of Women Voters and very active in the P.T.A. So many nights when I'd be moping in my room, I'd see her drive off to one meeting or another, and no one had a word but good to say about her. Every time I turned around I seemed to hear the name of Delia King, how wonderful she was.

Sometimes Mother and I would take a Sunday drive out to the farm stands for fresh vegetables. More than once we saw Lester and Delia walking by Greer Lake. He had his arm around her or they'd be holding hands with Davey running out ahead of them. If you'd told me then that in a few months he would leave her, I'd never have believed it. They looked the picture of a happy family, and I wondered if Delia even realized how lucky she was.

You'd almost think that suffering was something shameful, worse than sin, the way a person takes such pains to hide it and the way we think so highly of someone who triumphs over it. I remember how closely people watched Delia after Lester left her, and how relieved they were to see her go right on with life as if nothing had changed. She went off to her meetings, she taught her eighth grade students and she sang her solos with the choir. I remember those first few Sundays how such a silence built up in the church the moment she stood up to sing, as if the people all were straining hard to hear if there was something different in her voice. I watched her at the Lord's Prayer and the General Confession with her head bent and her eyes closed. The light from the sacristy caught the shine of her hair and fell on her head like my own wish or blessing. I watched her face until I saw that it was serious, but calm.

People said that Delia never mentioned Lester and I'm sure that no one said his name within her hearing, though he and his secretary, Dawn Sidelle, were the talk of town for quite a while. "Delia's better off without a man like that," her friends insisted. I said it, too, as if a little problem had been solved. Later on I realized that it wasn't quite that simple. Sleepless nights when I'd be up, I'd look across the street and see the light in Delia's bedroom burning brightly in the blackness. It was just a little square of light, but it said so much. I don't know why, but when I'd picture Delia in that lighted room, I'd always think her loneliness must be much worse than mine could ever be. And I don't know why her happiness ever mattered so much to me either. Some people's troubles hardly touch you. But maybe they're the ones who seem to earn them or deserve them. With someone like Delia there wasn't any justice to the things that happened to her.

Delia

In the six months he'd been gone, she'd learned never to think of Lester, though all his suits were hanging in his closet and all his underwear and shoes and socks and ties. He'd never come to claim a single one of his belongings, this man who'd called one night at dusk while she was cooking supper and announced, "I won't be coming home," in an odd, cold voice. "I've got to be on my own a while," was all he said.

She could find his cuff link on the floor and pick it up as if it had belonged to anyone, or stare from where she sat in bed across the room at his hair brush on the bureau, the one he'd used hundreds of times which held no imprint of him, offered not a single emanation of him. It was as if all of his things had dispossessed him. She could look at any one of them and her mind would grow completely empty, white, as if the shock Lester had given her was the only memory she had of him and all the rest were unreliable or false. The monthly checks she took as if they came out of the air, just for Davey's benefit. In those six months he'd never called her once or written to her or appeared.

"I couldn't face you. I was too ashamed," he said when he came back, standing on the lawn and looking up at her as if she were his judge. The stubble on his chin stood out in little spikes like weakness crying out for scorn.

"It's all my fault. Everything that's happened," he said repeatedly, almost with pride, bleary-eyed and lurching from the liquor, as if he revelled in his pain. Each day he came, always looking the same, until it seemed to Delia that there was no mystery left to him at all, this man who looked so miserable and small. She told herself that she felt nothing for him, yet each time he drove away she saw that she had held her breath, had hardly breathed the whole time he was there.

She quit her teaching job and all her town committee work and stayed at home. She spent her afternoons out on the porch with Davey. Her friends kept calling her at first, inviting her out, but she said she wouldn't dream of it until the boy was well. Toward the end of summer she began to take him out for walks. Sometimes they'd go six times around the block. She had to hold his hand because his co-ordination wasn't good and he had dizzy spells. Her skirts were all too tight from the weight she'd gained and she hadn't time to keep her hair as nice as it used to be. Long strands of it hung by her face, but she didn't seem to notice or to care. The neighbors stopped to stare when they went by— at the child whose eyes were empty, like a dead man's eyes, without any expression in them. When Delia said he was getting better all the time, they thought she was deluding herself and they wondered where it all would end.

The last time she saw Lester, he looked so bad she didn't have the heart to tell him she was moving. The house was up for sale, and she was taking Davey down to Florida to live where it was warm year round. She liked to think of all the water and the heat and how the child would be so dazzled by the sun.

Mary Taggard

My last year in high school the guidance counsellor, Mr. Brewster, asked me what my plans were after graduation. I said I didn't know. I supposed I'd get a job. "You ought to think about it very carefully," Mr. Brewster said. "There's a perfect job for everyone out there. You want to find the work that you were *meant* to do. Not just any job." I was surprised to see how concerned he was. I guess it showed, because he said, "You've no idea what a difference it makes, Mary. Your whole life makes sense if you love your work." I'd sit in his crowded office with his desk piled high with application forms and the pamphlets he kept handing me about the different careers. It touched me how much he seemed to care. He called me in a number of times that year, and he was always so enthusiastic that I could never bring myself to tell him that there wasn't any special job I wanted. I didn't care to go away to school either or to travel, even to leave home yet. I'd always thank Mr. Brewster for his trouble, carry away the pile of booklets that he gave me, and throw them in the trash when I'd get home. I never even looked at them.

After graduation I took my job at Federal Savings just the way my father went to work in road construction. I don't believe that he ever loved his job, but it gave him self-respect and a weekly pay check. About a month ago they threw a party for me at the bank. It was a total surprise. Mr. Deacon, our bank President, gave a little speech about what a fine, reliable worker I had always been, and he said he hoped I'd be happy with my new promotion to Assistant Manager in Charge of Loans. Everyone clapped. They brought in a tray of hors d'oeuvres and champagne. The women all came up to kiss me, and they laughed because I couldn't say a single word. I was just speechless.

I've been thinking a lot of Papa recently. He'll be gone three years this June. The other day I overheard Mother talking to her friend May Nesbitt on the phone. "Mary seems so much happier these days," she was saying. "I think it's taken her all this time to get over her father. It was a terrible blow to her the way he went so suddenly." I was miffed to hear Mother talking so freely about me, especially to May Nesbitt, who is a gossip, but I wondered if there was any truth to what she said. These past weeks I've been feeling so much better. I've started eating well again and I have no trouble sleeping. All the worry and the nerves have disappeared, and it happened just as suddenly as if I had been riding through a tunnel two years long and one day sailed out into the light. I enjoy the smallest thing, whether it's shopping with Mother or walking down the hill to work or reading the papers in the evening on the porch. I feel peaceful, and I can't imagine why, because nothing has changed. Nothing at all really. Sometimes I test this peaceful feeling to see if I can make it disappear. I tell myself that someday I'll lose Mother. How will I manage all alone, and won't my life seem pitiful and empty, just the saddest disappointment when I'm sixty and I look back on it? I ask myself the worst things I can think of, but they hardly seem to faze me or upset me. It's the strangest thing, and I don't expect I'll understand it any more than you can know exactly why you care so much for one person and so little for another. You just do.

Some people took the place across the street the moment Delia put it on the market. A young couple, Barbara and Jim Andrews —in their early thirties, I'd guess. He's a lawyer and she stays home with the children. They have a little boy and girl, they drive a station wagon, and they fit a certain mold so well, you know they'll keep the lawn cut and the bushes trimmed just so and that their lights will all go out by ten o'clock most nights. I notice them about as much as you would notice a tree outside your window. You know it's going to grow a certain way.

I often think of Delia. I think how Mother went to visit them so many times when Davey came home from the hospital, and how she took them soups she'd made and casseroles and pies, while I could never make myself go with her, though I knew I ought to. Mother could sit out on their porch in the burning sun and chat with them as if there was no heat and there had been no tragedy.

The morning Delia and Davey left town, there was quite a crowd to see them off. Mostly women friends of Delia's. The moving van carried off the contents of the house and Delia's car was packed up to the roof. Davey sat in the front seat. He sat so still, you hardly noticed him. He didn't say a word to anybody. He just stared ahead out the front window. Delia came out of the house and she looked so tired you could see how the past year had aged her. But she was wearing a pretty yellow suit which looked brand new and her hair was pinned up nicely. She went around to everyone and she kissed or hugged each one. You could see that she wanted to leave cheerfully and with no tears.

"You've been wonderful to us," she said when she came up to Mother and me.

"We'll miss you. The neighborhood won't be the same without you," Mother said. I could feel my own face burning crimson. Delia kissed each one of us on the cheek.

When she climbed into the car, she patted Davey on the shoulder, as if to tell him that the whole ordeal was nearly over. He turned to her with a small but eager look. It only lasted for a second, but it was as if a mask had lifted from his face and you could see that the old Davey was sitting right there even if he didn't know it yet himself.

We watched the car till it was just a speck of red at the end of our street. Even then we stood there for a while the way that people at the shore will sometimes stand and look out at the empty sea.

Three Vignettes

Group Therapy

"MY PROBLEM IS I can't have sex unless I'm reading," says the man with red hair.

"Oh? Well, I can't pray unless I'm smoking," says the pretty girl beside him. "And I'd like to be a nun."

"And I can't hold a conversation with anyone, even on the simplest level, unless all ten rooms in my house are spotless," says the woman with the print dress. "Otherwise I'm incapable of any logic."

"That's nothing. What about me?" asks the thin man with the flat face. "I can't laugh or even smile without getting a nose bleed. It happens every time. And it's a fine fix to be in, let me tell you. I haven't a friend in the world. I'd have to be anemic to be popular."

Other voices pipe up all around the circle. "I can't feel warm unless I'm really cold. There isn't a day all winter long when I'm not ill. I've had pneumonia four times."

"And I can't cry. Whenever I feel like crying, I start to laugh. I couldn't even go to my mother's funeral."

After everyone has spoken there is a heavy, aching silence as all eyes in the group turn to the little psychiatrist who sits at the center of the circle, a slim woman in a flowered dress of roses and camellias as gay and bright as her smile. "Oh, tell us, Dr. Joyce, how are you?" gasps the pretty girl who wants to be a nun. And all around the circle tension mounts. Dr. Joyce is wearing a new perfume, and the scent is so strong it might mean anything.

"I'm fine. Just perfect," says Dr. Joyce, and her laugh breaks over the group like a shower of confetti. "We had the most beautiful trip," she sighs, looking over their heads into space, as if she can see the long beach of sparkling sand and sea or the formal dining room by candlelight where the women wore white or shocking pink to set off their sun-flushed faces, and the men were almost as elegant and gracious as Mr. Joyce, though they didn't have his fire or his sense of humor. "Mr. Joyce was as charming as always," she says, shaking her head with disbelief, the way she does at all of her good fortune. "There wasn't a day when he didn't bring me flowers or a night when he didn't drink to me with one of his devastating toasts. To think that after fifteen years it still goes on. But I'm not sorry to be back," she says, returning to the room and basking a warm gaze on every face around her. "I missed you all. Did you get my cards?"

All of the tension is gone. The patients nod and smile, even the thin man, though it makes his nose bleed. Dr. Joyce hands him some flowered Kleenex from the box she keeps to the left of her tiny feet.

"Are the children well?" asks the woman with the clean house.

"Oh, very," says Dr. Joyce. "They met us at the plane. And when we got home, they'd cooked a special dinner, and the house was immaculate. I told Mr. Joyce I couldn't see what we'd ever *done* to deserve such children."

"And your mother?" asks the man with the red hair.

"She's wonderful. Very active and a delight to have in the house. There never was a woman I admired more than Mother."

"Will you be going home early today, Dr. Joyce?" asks the woman who can't cry.

"Yes, I've been spoiled to death for the past two weeks, and I *am* going home early to cook the best dinner I can think of— something that everybody likes."

"Would that be a roast, Dr. Joyce?" asks the man with the red hair.

"A roast would be perfect, Rodney. How did you ever guess?" she cries with a little ladder of laughter.

"We'll meet again on Thursday," says Dr. Joyce a half hour later, wrapped in a purple velvet coat, her arm around the waist of the girl who wants to be a nun. "I'm so happy to see you and

65

so glad to be back," she says, moving in circles while she speaks, nearly dancing to the door. "Good-by," she calls with a wave to the group, whose eyes have followed her like many-colored streamers all the way across the room.

Failures

Their faces chalk white, their muscles without tone, a little crowd of failures sits together in a warm group. "As long as none of us succeeds, we will all be happy," says one.

"As long as we remain on the same level, we will be able to have picnics together like this," says the one beside him, and all of them sigh together a sigh of shared misery and complete kinship.

"If I were to succeed," says one of them, "I would lose every friend I have. Oh, on the surface they might seem to love me just the same, but the more successful I became, the more aggressive and destructive towards me they would feel."

"Exactly," everyone agrees.

"And yet if you succeeded on a grand scale," ventures the only one in the group wearing a red bow tie, "If you became President' let's say, isn't it possible that you'd feel less pain and frustration than we do?" But all of the rest turn on him severely.

"It is best to fail," they all say in unison. "And the more you fail the better off you are."

"I couldn't agree more," says a man with a paunch the size of a beach ball. "There is nothing I look forward to more than my own death bed, where I expect to be surrounded at last by a ring of absolutely sincere faces full of the kind of unconditional love I've longed for all of my life."

"Yes," says a man with a pimpled nose. "After infancy it's probably nearly impossible for a man to be so loved again until the moment of his passing."

"How many times we've been over this subject," says the man with the bow tie. "And look at these sandwiches. Have you ever seen anything more unappetizing? The meat is spoiled and the bread is stale. Can't we even enjoy a successful meal?" he says,

66

snapping a twig in two. "I'm fed up, I really am. Do you see that tree?" he asks, pointing to a scrubby pine in the distance. "I'm going to beat all of you to the top of it," he says with a leering challenge in his voice. And jumping to his feet, he begins to run away from the group.

"How childish and ridiculous," says the man with the paunch, as two other men from the group spring up to join the race.

"Don't follow him," cries the little crowd. But the two men, while they run, are kicking up their heels. Already their cheeks are bright pink.

"It's a delight to get off the ground, isn't it?" asks one of them.

"Yes," replies the other. "In a way, I wish we'd never reach the tree."

Those who remain behind in a white heap scorn the runners in tones of great disgust. Yet all the while out of the corners of their eyes they watch the three competitors who now tear up the hill toward the base of the tree in the last burst of the race.

"What fools they are," says the group, and everyone has a hearty laugh at the scrambling bunch. The bow-tied runner, who has kept the lead with little effort, swings up over the bottom branch of the tree with a surprising show of energy well before the others arrive. Yet he never slows his pace. The staring group falls silent as he pulls himself up branch after branch until he has reached the top.

"I've won! I've won!" he cries in such a tone of shocking exuberance, some of the failures feel a little weepy. One can't help but applaud. "I'll have to admit," he says, "that I'm terribly moved. I really long to join him in the tree."

Soon they are all making their way slowly up the hill and into the tree until the tree is full of them.

"I won," cries each one of them when he reaches the top. Then the one below him pushes him out of the tree to take his turn at the pinnacle. They all climb and then fall until the ground is covered with them.

"At least we all will have died triumphantly," each one of them says before he hits the ground. Finally there is silence. Only the man with the paunch who was unable to climb the tree is left.

He stands transfixed, staring at the prone crowd. Then he begins to cry. "All of my friends are dead," he says, and he is convulsed with terrible sobs and sighs for a long while. Then, shaking his head, with his hands on his hips, he begins to laugh. For twenty minutes his whole body shakes with violent mirth. He falls on the ground exhausted. When he wakes up, he discovers that his stubborn paunch has been agitated to the size of a volley ball. He is thrilled. He turns his back on his friends, and with dreamy anticipation he trots away towards a new and glorious vision of himself that hangs suspended like a carrot before his nose.

Manners

As a child she was taught few manners. As an adolescent she thinks that manners are stagey, silly. She never says 'please' and very rarely 'thank-you.' She believes in being direct. None of this pussy-footing around. "Pass the salt, will you?" gets the point across. So does a blunt "shut up" to the people who won't stop talking at the movies. "I like getting older," she says, smart and cocky. "The older you get the less you care what people think or how you impress them."

Once, though, she is polite. To a drunk who yanks her off the street into a black alley late at night. "Please," she manages to say, as the man presses a knife to her throat.

"Sit down," he orders, pointing to an orange crate. Wild-eyed, he offers her a cigarette.

"Yes, thank-you," she says, prim with terror, sitting on the crate. She restrains herself from asking his intentions, and while she smokes he sits across from her on the bottom rung of a fire escape. She can't see his face in the dark, but she can smell his liquored breath. She thinks he must be watching her, preparing to attack. She sits absolutely still, barely breathing, until she hears him begin to snore. He has fallen asleep. Pulling herself up, she tiptoes right past him, her movements terse and terrified, as if her whole body were crying "Excuse me, please excuse me" all the way up the alley.

Ned

—for S.H.

NOT ONCE IN FORTY YEARS have I gone without a meal or slept without a roof over my head. I've known less deprivation than anyone I know. My father died two months before I was born, it is true, and my daughter passed away before she ever spoke a word. But it's hard to miss what you never knew. I was my mother's only child. For twenty years we lived together. Her death was the greatest loss I ever suffered. Four months after she was buried, I was married to a girl I'd known since childhood. I couldn't live without a woman in the house.

My life is not much different now than it ever was. Mary and I live in the house I was born in. I've eaten every breakfast I can remember in the kitchen and most of my noon meals right here in this dining room. Right now I'm finishing my lunch, about to take my afternoon nap as soon as I finish the editorial page. Just about the time the clock in the living room strikes one, I will go to my room. Mary is in the kitchen baking bread with her sister Louise. She hardly ever has her lunch with me. Half the time she isn't home in the middle of the day. She always has a committee or a board meeting, a hair appointment or a friend she has to see. Which suits me fine. After a long morning's work, I like to be alone. I'm up before five six mornings a week. As a boy I had a paper route, and now I deliver mail to the same families, the only postman in Aston, because the town is so small. In a year I hardly see an unfamiliar face. The town, which is nearly self-sufficient, has nothing to offer a tourist. There are a few travelling salesmen that pass through, and once in a while a young couple looking for land. But nobody ever buys land in Aston. What isn't owned has gone to swamp.

Now, over the top of the newspaper, I see exactly what I'd expect. The window to my left captures the front view of the tool barn with the doors neatly barred shut. Out of sight inside the barn sits my green pick-up in perfect running condition with barely a scratch on it after two years' hard use. I know as much about cars as I do about birds and coins, though Mary always says it amazes her how I seem to know something about everything.

Out of the window on my right Mary's flower garden is prettier than any painting a man could want on his wall. Everyone who comes to the house comments on the garden. She's the queen of the county when it comes to flowers. I laid the brick walks and built the trellises for her roses twenty years ago, just after we were married.

The living room clock chimes one, and I push back from the sunny table, leaving my napkin folded on the fork side of my plate. Mary will clear the table in a few minutes, and I will fall asleep to the noise of my dishes in the sink. Normally I'd say a word to Mary before going upstairs. But I've never been comfortable with Louise. She's a nervous, giddy woman, a spinster who is ill-at-ease with men. I rise, staring at the barn. "I've taken a nap every afternoon for thirteen years and never had a sick day in all of that time," I used to tell people, as if I'd found the secret to success. I was about as modest as a peacock in those days, though I tried to keep my vanity to myself. I never mentioned how fond I was of my routine or the way I nurtured all of the rituals of my daily life with the same care I lavished on my dogs, the houseplants, my work and my relations with my wife. I thought I had good reason to be proud. All of the rest of Aston people appeared to be afflicted with disease and death, alcoholism, adultery, divorce or suicide. I took full credit for my happiness, as if I'd earned it. I liked my schedule to run as neatly as my pick-up truck. When I had my way, Mary would appear on the doorstep at the stroke of four. "I suppose you're getting hungry, Ned," she'd say, looking in the hall mirror while she took off her hat and fluffed out her hair. I would have liked that scene to be repeated every day. But Mary wasn't the predictable kind. I never knew what time she'd be home, at which door she'd appear, or what her humor would be. This used to bother me.

The pleasure of the journey from the lunch table to my room is the familiar trail of rugs, the paintings and the furniture that hug the walls like faithful spectators to a daily parade. My view is wallpapered the whole way to the stairs with jays and nuthatches and sparrows from floor to ceiling pecking in the snow. All of the shocks and surprises of my life, even mother's death and the baby's, and all of Mary's sudden moods and whims have not been enough to make me believe that I won't find my room exactly the way I'd expect it to be, and that in lying down there will be no texture of the bedspread or blanket, no temperature of my pillow, no sound or odor in the air that will be strange or unaccounted for. "I don't like surprises," I used to say. I learned the name of every flower, tree, animal and stone on my land. And I collected as many certainties, rules, laws (and their exceptions) as I could apply to all of the people and objects I knew, well beyond the truths of my bedspread, pillow, or property, as far as the weather that contained the county like a womb. Where rain, wind, sun, hot or cold were as well known to me as my body. Certain days I used to lie down as if everything for a hundred miles were part of me.

Pulling down the shades to the sound of my dishes in the kitchen, I take off my shoes and shirt, and sink with a sigh to the bed. The warm air blowing across my face through the window left open a crack carries the muffled voice of Louise and the fragrance of Mary's flowers intertwined. "I don't like surprises," I could repeat, lounging like an infant in the arms of the day. And yet, having reviewed my plans for the afternoon and evening, feeling free of worry, clean as an empty sky, I think of last night. How I lay in bed waiting for Mary, wanting her company more than usual, and the way I felt my love for her grow until my mind could not contain it, and the thought spilled over, filling my body with longing. And just as I was predicting what her face would be when she entered the room and imagining the way I'd kiss her cheek which would be cool and smell of lemon cologne,

I heard her crying. She was in the bathroom staring at herself in the mirror. "I can't believe it's me, Ned," was all she said. I knew what she was thinking, but I was surprised. Mary has always taken care of her appearance and kept herself as clean and neat as she keeps the house. But never seemed to set much store by her looks. Whenever I've complimented her on a dress or a hair-do, or told her that she "looked like a million" on some special occasion, she's smiled the same way she does when I'm pleased with one of her pies. Nothing more. Last night, even after I held her and told her she was more beautiful to me than she'd ever been, I wasn't sure I'd convinced her. She fell asleep in my arms and I lay awake, kissing her face sometimes, because I've never been good at putting my feelings in words. And I remembered a girl I knew nearly twenty-two years ago, who cried out my name when I made love to her. I can still remember her face, the way it hid nothing. So much love was there that all of my defenses fell, and I was never so free with any woman again. I never thought of marrying Blanche Faber. It didn't occur to me. But because of Blanche I know that Mary is responsible for the shyness that comes over me whenever I want to open my heart to her or shower her with praises. She's embarrassed by emotions.

Louise and Mary are laughing. They are very close. Louise knows how to make Mary laugh the way nobody else can. She is five years older, a school teacher, and one of the better educated people in town. Mary would have gone to college, too, if she hadn't married me instead. Sometimes I think Louise resents me for this. Like everyone else she probably wonders why I never amounted to much. My teachers used to say I was the brightest pupil they'd ever had, and my mother predicted a great future for me. I surprised everyone when I said I didn't want to go to college. I had no ambition to leave our town or join a profession. I liked my life just the way it was, and my only dream was to have it continue exactly the same. There are those who will say it's travel, new acquaintances, and new experiences that teach you about life. I always felt that to leave home, take a demanding job and live with strangers in alien surroundings would only distract me from the little that I knew. I got no encouragement in my decision to stay at home. But I was as stubborn then as I am now. I've always had a closed mind, and liked the questions best that I know the answers to, and been unshakeable in a few convictions. My arguments made as little sense to my mother as they do to Mary, who'd take a trip every week if we could afford it. She and Louise travel together every year. They've been as far as Canada and Bermuda. Now they want to go to Spain. Mary nags me to go with her, but I never have. When I tell her how bored I'd be, she looks at me as if I'm crazy, and says she wouldn't want to live if she didn't have something to look forward to. Some nights she paces through the house as if it were a cage. Always busy with never enough to do. It's the disappointment of her life not having children. After the first one the doctor said she couldn't have more. When our baby died, Mary said: "I've never loved anything so much." She was hysterical when she said this, but I've never forgotten it, and often wondered if she didn't mean it. I never shed a tear for the baby. If I suffered it was only for Mary, who hardly spoke to me for four months, as if she guessed how little the child had meant to me and resented me for it. I didn't try to defend myself. Mary wouldn't have understood. I'd have hurt her if I'd told her the truth; that I wasn't in love with her at the time I married her, though I admired her more than any girl in town, and just as I couldn't suffer for a heartless infant that had never spoken a word did I now cherish Mary more than ever and love her to a degree that might dismay her if she knew. Why wouldn't I love her more now in middle age, when the pattern of her habits is coming into focus like a map? She's developed a texture and an odor all her own. The older she grows, the more she becomes, the more I love her. If I could understand her I think there would be little left to bother me. I enjoy my work and feel as much at home on any street in Aston as I do in this room. I have no enemies or close friends, but everyone in town is a warm acquaintance. I make an effort to keep all of my relations with people good, just the way good food, good music or fine weather is better than bad, even if Mary is the only one that matters to me. Oh, there are some days, when

I pass Ike Brainard's place at the end of my route, and I envy him, living like a hermit with twenty cats for company and no woman to throw a wrench in his plans for a quiet evening or rankle a mood of his with one of hers. Sometimes I wonder if my life wouldn't have been completely peaceful if I'd lived alone and cared for no one. I never knew what loneliness was till after I was married.

Last night, after she was asleep, I looked at Mary's face as hard as I could, to see what had upset her in the mirror. Her hair is thinning, her forehead is lined, and her frown lines are pronounced. She frowns often, whether she's writing a letter or reading a book—whenever she thinks. In sleep she doesn't look like herself, because she's normally never still. She's a small woman. Her mouth is as small as a child's. The lips were turned down at the corners as if she were still disturbed in her sleep. During the day she appears larger. I'd say she's one of the most admired women in town, president of her clubs and active in all civic affairs. She's always had a power with people. They like to please her and they like to win her approval. People trust her. She is not a gossip, and she takes authority as naturally as a queen. Her expression is usually thoughtful. Her eyes are very blue and lively, but you can't know what she's thinking till she speaks her mind. She doesn't smile often so that when she does it gives more pleasure than a smile usually does. Whenever she smiles I feel my heart lift at the sight of it. Sometimes I think she has the power to conduct my feelings like a band with the slightest changes in her face. Her skin is very soft, and the color in her cheeks is always high (on account on her high blood pressure, she says). The combination of her dark hair and her bright cheeks gives her a striking, healthy look. I suppose she is no beauty, but I'm the last one able to judge her appearance.

The smell of fresh baked oatmeal bread is rising through the house the way I knew it would. It is a soothing smell but I can't sleep today. I doubt if there's another man in Aston, married for twenty years, that wonders so much about his wife, as if she were the greatest mystery in his life. But then I've always been so far removed from Aston people there might as well have been a

74

chasm between us. From a distance they've looked at me affectionately, particularly since I married Mary. I never was very social. As a boy in school I was friendly enough, but I preferred to spend my time alone. I suppose my classmates thought I was aloof, but it was generally accepted I was the town genius, which naturally set me apart. "You were so serious and so much more refined than all the rest, there wasn't another boy in town that ever impressed me so much," Mary's said many times. My mother always worried that I must be lonely, which I never was. Afternoons, whenever the weather allowed it, I hid myself in the high grass behind the house in the shade of the old elm tree that is still there today. On my stomach I would lie as long as it took until the stillness of the field came over me. I envied the elm, rooted to one spot, with all of its needs met by the earth and sky. I was sure that time would disappear if I, too, were able to remain there forever, staring at the same view. First the future would go, as quickly as it takes to switch off a bright lamp, then the past would fade, until in its full glory, the present would overpower me like a drug. It was as if I'd tasted reality once and hungered for it like an addict ever since. I'd watch the sun fall behind the trees and feel a chill rising in the ground and air. The smell of fried chicken or roast pork would often escape the house and drift across the yard until I'd rise to answer my mother's call before she even summoned me to dinner. And hurry like an outcast toward the house, as if it were a prison that I craved. When a boy is cold and hungry, can he think of anything else? I realized early that my comforts were important to me. I believed the more you made a man comfortable, the more you satisfied the little needs that distracted him, the more he approached the stillness of an elm. Now I know there's no limit to a man's desires and no end to his needs.

One night, two years ago, when I made love to Mary, I could see that she enjoyed it and wasn't doing it to please me the way she usually does. Her whole face was so changed, I was transfixed by it. I couldn't look at her enough. Her eyes that normally would have been averted, gazed at me so openly that looking into them I saw there was no end to her. The more I looked at her, the more

I saw her soul, as clearly as I can see the yellow threads of this blanket today. It was as if by accident she had revealed to me the face she regularly presents to God. (She is a devout Christian.) "This is the part of you I always wanted and never knew was there," I could have said to her. But I was afraid to speak, as if the spell of the moment were too delicate for words. I understood jealousy when I imagined anyone else could ever see her so naked. I felt so close to her that I wept, a thing I hadn't done since my mother's death. She held me and said, "Oh, Ned" in a soft voice, but I knew it upset her to see me so moved. I lay in her arms like a lovesick boy, I who had never believed in falling in love. When I was seventeen or eighteen I used to think it wouldn't matter much who I married. The people I cared about were the ones I knew well. The better I knew them the more I cared. Oh, I still believe you'd have to love anyone you'd known so well and so long as I've known Mary, but the passion I discovered that night must be reserved for a select few whose beauty we perceive with the same longing the Lord is said to have for our souls.

Though I expected that night would change our lives together, the next day was like any other. Mary behaved as if nothing had happened. She was surprised how often I wanted to make love to her in the next weeks, and even expressed disapproval, as if it weren't seemly for people our age to carry on so. There wasn't ever a night like that again. Sometimes I've blamed myself for frightening her and sometimes I've thought I must have dreamed the whole thing. Whatever happened, I wasn't the same after it. The more I longed to recapture that moment with Mary, the more it became the greatest happiness I could imagine. I saw that my whole life had been a striving after intimacy, and that before that night I'd felt as confident as a king on his way to conquering the world. I knew the way my coffee would taste in the morning before I ever tasted it, and what the gravel would sound like under my feet (depending on the weather) before I even started out the driveway. At the age of thirty-eight, I approached the town of Aston as if all of its houses, faces, voices, animals, trees, odors, and colors waited to confirm my memory and my expectation of them. The sight of each mail box pleased me the way that any certainty delighted me. Many mornings, when I started my route, I felt ecstatic, as if around each bend the road already lay as perfectly paved in my mind as the one I would find in the world. By the time I returned home I was smug enough that Mary's moods hardly fazed me. I had seen them all before and even imagined there must be a cycle to them that I would decipher someday. Given time and concentration, I imagined there was nothing that wouldn't make itself plain to me eventually.

The more I pursued Mary, the more my ardour embarrassed and irritated her. It was as if my passion, once born, could only grow. My longing for her extended like a flame that burned all the way back to my childhood until it covered every inch of my experience and revealed the shallowness and the self-importance and the smugness of it. Mary spent more time away from the house. When she was home we quarrelled more than we ever had in our marriage. I could imagine her saying to a friend, "I don't know what's gotten into Ned. Do you think it could be middle age?" though I knew there wasn't a soul with whom she'd discuss her private life. I could see that I was hurting and confusing her with my daily and nightly demands. It seemed to me that she stood in the way of my happiness like a wall. Yet it also seemed the moment I stopped pursuing her and resigned myself to accepting her the way she was that she became affectionate again, more than she'd ever been before. There was a day about six months ago when she kissed me three times and told me that she loved me.

Yesterday I saw my hammer in a way that made me know I'd never seen it before, a hammer that I've owned for thirty years. I wasn't disturbed. I've grown accustomed to surprises. Along my route I've tried to anticipate every unexpected change I might discover, the way I used to watch predictions for the weather. And I wouldn't be surprised if the boulder over the road just before the McKinnon's place rolled out of its niche some morning and nearly crushed me as it bounced across my way. One Monday, when I found that John Eldridge had painted his barn

77

a bright red over the weekend, razed his tool shed, and put up window boxes for his wife Lil's flowers, I didn't give it a second thought. I wouldn't have been surprised if all of Aston had been razed or painted red. Well, that's not true. But I'm getting near that point.

There are weeks when I can hardly see the houses or the people on my route for the cloud of memories that overcomes me. And days like today when I say, what right or reason have I to suffer when I've had so much and lost so little. Why do I lie here hardly able to hear the birds above the din of fear and longing in my body? Maybe it's middle age. Mary says I need a change of scene. There are times when the thought of an unknown city in another country appeals to me, as if the choices of my life had been mistakes and all of my deepest yearnings had been foolish. I tell myself I'd let her pick the place and how we'd get there. I wouldn't study guide books and I'd go as unprepared and ignorant as I could, anticipating nothing. And if I had my way my mind would be as empty as a mirror that only reflects the moment it is in.

But I hold onto my habits like a bull dog, no matter how I'm shaken, like an inventor who is stymied for the moment or a religious man whose faith is being tested, as if I'm on the verge of understanding. As if one day at lunch I'll see the tool barn shift on its foundation and hear it heave the sigh of patient satisfaction that I've expected of it since I was a boy, when I used to stare at the birds on the wall paper in the hall, defying them to move, and when the longer I stared the more frightfully real they became, until my courage failed me and I turned away, as if I had the power to bring the whole inanimate world to life if I dared to give it my passionate concentration.

The clock in the living room is striking two. I may as well get up. Louise is leaving. Mary is walking her out to her car, speaking in a low voice, not to waken me. Mary is a considerate person, considerate of everyone. But it touches me, her whispering.

The Success and the Little Failure

THE LITTLE FAILURE was crying softly. Her tears that never ceased streamed steadily down from tiny eyes across her cheeks, which were chapped all winter. She had a clenched, little face, a strangely pimpled nose, and a swollen little mouth that never took a natural shape. Even now the corners of the lips turned down into a triangle of such exaggerated misery, the soft-hearted success had to laugh in spite of himself. It was an affectionate laugh, but the little failure, ever suspicious and always on the defensive, stopped to scrutinize his face, shocked at the possibility of some new kind of mockery. Finding the old warmth in the eyes of the success, she began to cry again. "Well, at least I'm relaxed," she said, as she always did whenever he rebuked her. "If I weren't relaxed, I wouldn't be able to cry," she said, looking up at the success, whose beauty always amazed her. Now, in the middle of the day, she could give him only a quick appraisal. At night, long after he'd fallen asleep, she studied him closely. Sometimes she sat till dawn beside him, gazing at his immense proportions, his feet which stretched so far beyond the end of their bed, his skin her own dream of such smooth perfection, she had to remind herself more than once not to touch his flesh. She watched him white by moonlight, then in the grey light until the sun dawned on him and rose glinting in his gold watch. He wore gold well. Even his wiry hair sparkled gold, picked up every highlight until it gave off a light of its own, she was sure, and cast a little shadow of gold all around his head on the pillow. His enormous face was what she looked at most. Those colossal eyes of which she never lost her fear, into which she never looked directly, though she could remember them perfectly even when they were closed, lashed down so heavily it seemed they would

79

never open again. Was there ever a nose so large, yet dignfied and ruler straight, or a mouth so mammoth? Such a sensuous but always sensitive mouth most often gentle in its huge expression. Yes, he was magnificent, she told herself more than once on many nights, whenever she studied him.

"But we've sat here long enough," said the success, who liked activity and never rested till he went to sleep. It was a Sunday afternoon and they were sitting in the park. "What would it be fun to do?" he asked, asking himself really. It rarely mattered to the little failure what they did. But the success liked to be inspired as well as stimulated. There was nothing he liked better than to praise, and he would have been happy to live in a state of perpetual awe. His vocabulary was full of ecstatic exclamations. "Superb," "incredible," and "gorgeous" were words he often used glancing up from a book, walking out of a concert, leaving a restaurant or looking up at the sky.

The little failure was just the opposite. Cries of praise were out of the question. In fact she rarely spoke at all. Every admirable thing in the world made her sad. The more impressive the painting, the poem, the person, the more she wept. In the presence of a masterpiece she could become nearly hysterical. When the success turned to her with rapture at the end of some performance, or as they drove away from a party of lively, laughing people, he never expected to find upon her face any expression other than the usual, and only planted one of his many kisses on her drenched face and told her that her tears were delicious.

There was no doubt that he loved her. To all of the many people who called themselves his friends and visited the house, this was an obvious fact, though difficult to understand. What he saw in his miserable, frowzy wife was beyond them. Sullen and unkempt, she was not the friend of any one of them and rarely had a word and never a smile to extend. Yet the success was continually delighted with her, and had no eyes for any other woman. When she presented to their guests a tray of burnt hors d'oeuvres, he said "What a boob you are," as if he had never been more charmed. While he spoke to his friends, she often sat with downcast eyes in the crook of his arm. And many a night, after a number of drinks, tears would come to his eyes as he looked down at her and said "I wouldn't know what to do without her" in a way that made all other eyes in the room rest briefly, even enviously on her with a kind of tenderness she never inspired at any other time.

The success loved to sleep. He approached his bed as if he were about to fling himself into the delicious depths of the sea. He fell immediately into a deep sleep with a look of pleasure on his face. Or so it seemed to the little failure, who hated sleep. She put it off till dawn, then fell unwillingly into a stupor. For an hour or so her little body arched and twitched. Teeth grinding, she sometimes battled wildly, emitting little cries of dismay at her dreams. This never woke the success, but he threw out a heavy arm across her and pinned her still. She awoke in the morning, half sick and shrinking from the light, discovered his arm, looked at his huge palm, which was always open and fully extended, and she felt ashamed. Then he held her against his great chest and buried his nose in her grey gown while she smelled his sweet fragrance with her eyes tight shut. "You look so tired," he'd say, looking into her puffed face until the triangle took shape on her mouth. "Open your eyes," he'd insist, and when she did, she always began immediately to cry.

"Forgive me," the little failure was often tempted to say. "Forgive me for being so ugly," she wanted to cry. But nothing angered the success more than her own self-criticism. When she apologized for her looks, her tears, her continual mistakes, he found it unbearable, attacked her with a fury, and told her in various ways what he always told her; that he loved her for herself exactly as she was. The little failure could believe in his love, but because she couldn't find a single reason for it, it never really touched her. His love weighed upon her and made her wonder. What if she were ever, when he kissed her, to return his kiss? What if she were to smile or laugh just once with a perfectly dry face? What if in lovemaking, when she felt her limbs begin to follow his, if she were to respond in any way? But when the little failure wondered such things she had only to think of how many times he'd said, "Don't you see that I wouldn't *want* you if you were any different," and fear would turn her rigid as a fork, even while she was still tempted to ask, "If you love me so much, why won't you let us have a child?"

The success dressed in the finest clothes. Also he had an appetite for the most choice food and drink. His tastes were expensive but not disparate with his large income. He was a stellar lawyer who approached his profession with zest, played his work as well as he played every sport he took up. For all of his intelligence he rarely indulged in feelings of despair. But twice a year, usually in January and July, he retreated behind the locked doors of his house and spent at least a week in a state of wretchedness and gloom. His friends, who would not have recognized him, were not allowed to see him. His wife was the only one with whom he shared this twist of his personality.

She could see the signs of his depressions coming on. "I've turned on every light in the house, and still it looks so bleak," he would say at night. Putting a piece of his favorite music on the stereo, he turned the volume up and up until the house shook, but still the music didn't move him. Everything bored him, and whatever he normally admired he now began to criticize. The more critical he became, the more furious he grew until he'd found fault with every part of his life and every friend he had. After he had worn out all of his anger and expressed every bit of his disgust, he fell exhausted into bed where he lay for days unshaven and pale, speaking paragraphs to the ceiling as much as to his wife who never left his side. "Nothing makes me more ashamed than my own misery," he was likely to say. "The degree of a man's misery is the measure of his stupidity."

Listening to his harangues, the little failure was never more composed. During these black periods in their lives, she barely shed a tear. She also spoke more than she did at any other time and had no trouble finding the right vocabulary to cheer him. With warmth and sympathy she spoke, though his suffering left her cold. (Once when he was drunk, he lost his footing and fell down four flights of stairs while she watched and laughed.) She had no pity for him but took great pains to restore him, as if he were a painting of tremendous value or a piece of glorious music badly played. She wanted to smooth away his twisted expression with her hands.

"You're only in a mood," she'd say. "By next week you'll feel completely different."

As she predicted, there came a morning when the success woke up, lay for a moment dazzled, breathed in the shaft of cold air that swept across their sunny bed. "Open your eyes," he commanded, as if he were conducting an orchestra. "Have you ever smelt such air?" he asked in a voice that reached her like a signal. Even before she lifted her lids, her cheeks were damp.

"Let's take the subway to Lancaster Museum," said the success. There's supposed to be a great exhibit." They headed for the nearest subway station. "It's a perfect day," he said, steering his wife across the street so they could walk in the sun.

On the subway platform the little failure noticed a man whose behavior was unusual. A short, dark man with an Italian face, dressed in a striped suit which looked brand new. In one hand he carried a black hat and in the other he twirled a shiny, black cane. His face was serious while he twirled the cane as if it were a majorette's baton. He twirled it with such skill and such increasing speed, it was soon hard to see anything but a blur of it. Several people watched him from a distance, but when he threw the cane high in the air and caught it spinning behind his back, everyone on the platform stared at him. The man paid no attention to anyone. The longer they waited for the train, the more frenetic his behavior became. Several times he jumped up and down with impatience, it seemed. Jumped amazingly high for his own height and straight up in the air. Then whirled like a dancer the whole length of the platform with his cane extended, still unaware of the people who leapt out of his way. He had the bearing and the style of a performer, but his face was grave.

"Now there's a real nut," said the success, but the little failure was fascinated, held her breath. When the subway arrived, they stepped aboard and had just taken their seats when the little man bounded into their car. The success studied his own reflection in the window, but the little failure watched the Italian, who tapped his cane so hard against the floor, it seemed likely to break. Five times he jumped up to touch the roof of the car with his finger-tips. Then in a burst of impatience, he threw down his cane and ran the whole length of the car, not once uttering a sound or changing the expression on his face. The people shrank away, all eyes averted from the terrible sight. Back and forth he ran, his speed increasing all of the time, until it seemed to the little failure that she had never seen a man move so fast. He flung himself against one end of the car and threw himself back toward the other as if he were a swimmer in a desperate race. The little failure was so awed, she found herself standing up as if in tribute. "I've never seen anything like him," she said. The success, surprised by her voice and her flushed face, tugged her arm and tried to pull her to her seat. But she shook off his hand and only noticed him when she heard his angry whisper, "For God's sake, sit down."

"I will not," she loudly replied, and she looked straight into her husband's eyes. For a moment they stared at each other, and the little failure was dry-eyed and amazed at the abashed face of the success. Pinned on his eyes, she searched for some reflection of herself. But he mirrored nothing. His face went blank, he remained silent, and finally turned his eyes away, embarassed. She gaped at him while the madman thudded his cane. Triumphant, she turned her face on everyone in the car. The power of her expression made each person start or look away. She found her husband staring at his shoe. He didn't see the look of tenderness which glazed her eyes as in her mind she took him in her arms. So gently did she touch him, she hardly believed it was possible to be so gentle. And her kiss was so passionate, she felt her face and neck grow warm. She imagined them in the dark, and fell into his arms so fully, hot and aching, she trembled where she stood. She surrendered to every longing, fearlessly conceived their child, and carried it for nine months while her husband watched his shoe as if it were all that existed.

When the subway stopped, the success stood stiffly, actually waited for her to lead them out of the car. She steadied him as

84

the little Italian pushed past them, letting out such a terrific cry of relief, the moving crowd came to a halt, stepped back to make him an aisle down which they watched him run all the way to the stairs. The little failure, her fantasy shattered, watched him, too, while he shot up three flights, burst through the doors, and flung himself over the top with a high leap. She saw him in mid-air, flashing his cane in the sun, before he streaked out of sight, doors banged behind him, all askew.

The people sighed or laughed until they were composed. The success and the little failure followed behind in silence. Straight to the museum they went without a word. The face of the success was so pale. Seeing this, the little failure felt her mouth quiver toward a triangle. Her eyes grew small, brimmed with expectation as they climbed the museum steps. The success was smiling down at her, amused. "Well, at least I'm relaxed," she said, averting her eyes. "If I weren't relaxed, I wouldn't be able to cry," she said self-righteously.

A Strange Elation

BILL HALSEY TURNED to the obituary page, and there, as he'd expected, was a photograph of Lydia Peacham, their neighbor from across the street. Born in Cleveland, graduated with high honors from Smith College, a graphics artist whose work had won awards and prizes, she was dead of cancer at the age of thirty-three. She left a husband, Joseph, and a sister, Susan Escher, of Lake Forest, Illinois. The photograph looked dated and did not, Bill Halsey thought, do justice to the woman. He could still see Lydia Peacham's long-stemmed legs in a pair of shorts while she worked around her yard, the blonde hair swinging by her face, and the mysterious smile when he'd passed her on the road or in the town. She'd been the kind of woman he'd admired from a distance all of his life, but never dared to know or to pursue.

Bill Halsey sighed. He dropped the paper in a heap beside his chair and glanced about him. He was sitting in his living room. His daughters, Anne and Tracy, were lying on their stomachs on the rug. They still wore their church clothes, matching plaid skirts, white blouses, black patent leather shoes, and there were red ribbons in their tightly braided yellow hair. The sight of them was sweet to him. The sun came through the picture window making a definite square on the clean yellow rug. He could feel the warmth of it on his daughter's backs and on their small shoulders. They were coloring. He wanted to call them over to him, to hug their bendy little bodies and make their eyes flash with delight. But the older girl, Tracy, was humming while she worked, a tuneless chanting sound of lost contentment. He couldn't bring himself to interrupt her.

From the kitchen came the sounds of Laura cooking and the

86

smells of lamb and roast potatoes for their Sunday dinner. It was a mild fall day. The front door was wide open to the quiet, tree-lined street of wide-lawned houses, and a pleasant breeze, sharp with the smell of leaves, came into the room. He stretched and stood up, a thin, balding man with glasses, wearing a white, unwrinkled shirt and a red and green checked bow tie. He was thirty-nine, a dentist with a practice that had tripled in the past three years. He made his patients laugh. From the day he'd opened up his office he had joked with everyone who sat down in the plush white chair. It was as if he had no control over the jaunty tone of his own voice and the jokes, the anecdotes and cracks which poured out of his mouth all day with an abundance and variety that often amazed him. He wondered where they came from. He wasn't a "card" or a "comedian," as people often called him. Bill Halsey wondered whether, left to himself, he'd ever laugh at all.

He'd tried to explain it to Laura once, how his behavior at the office bothered him. One night in bed he'd tried to tell her. It was one of those nights when he knew that he wouldn't sleep for hours. And while the minutes ticked away, the day ahead would loom with frightful clarity, and he would clearly see the crowded waiting room of wan, expectant faces.

"I wish to God I didn't have to go to that office tomorrrow," he'd said quite suddenly to Laura in the dark, and hearing the truth of the words expressed aloud, he'd found himself in tears. He'd put his hands up to his face and wept, a thing he hadn't done in years. And switching on her light, Laura had seemed dumbfounded.

"Why, Bill?" She'd almost whispered the words.

"Because I hate the place, that's why," he'd said with a viciousness that gave him strange relief, almost a pleasure to see his wife so stunned. "You've no idea, Laura, what a luxury it is to be yourself. Just to be *yourself*," he'd almost shouted. Then, still weeping, through harsh sobs, he had described to her the hypocrite that she had never seen, the foolish clown that he became for eight straight hours every day.

"This has been going on for years, Laura. For *years*," he'd cried almost accusingly. But in the middle of his anger, when he'd felt that he'd just begun and that he could go on unburdening himself for hours, he'd suddenly been stopped dead by the sight of Laura's face, who'd looked at him uncomprehendingly and with fear, as if she'd been waked up to find the house in flames and now was watching it burn down to ruins. He'd never seen her look so frightened, and all of his anger had disappeared in the need to comfort her. He'd put his arms around her and found that she was shaking, trembling all over.

"Oh, Bill," was all that she'd said, and she'd begun to cry herself, strangely and bitterly like a child.

"I'm tired, honey. I'm just tired," he'd kept repeating. "I swear I didn't mean a word I said." Laura had fallen asleep in his arms, and since then she had never mentioned or referred to anything about that night.

There was a new yellow cloth on the dining room table and a centerpiece of daffodils and yellow roses in a silver bowl.

"Those look pretty," he said to Laura, who was sitting down, patting her hair in place, her face flushed from the kitchen. The girls were already seated in their chairs.

"Hurry, Daddy. Everything is getting cold," said Tracy, imitating Laura.

"All right, sweety," he said, taking his seat, and he leaned across to kiss her small round cheek.

"I forgot to tell you. Arthur Varnum called this morning," Laura said, shaking out her napkin. "He said he'd call back later."

Before him was the roast, ready to carve, a dish of green mint jelly, a pitcher of brown gravy, a platter of potatoes, and several bowls of steaming vegetables.

"For what we are about to receive, Lord, make us truly thankful," Laura said in the solemn voice that she reserved for prayers. "And please bless Lydia Peacham who died this week," she added.

He'd planned to spend the afternoon raking the yard, but after the heavy dinner he felt sleepy. The girls had disappeared out-

88

doors and the house was peaceful. He stretched out on the couch. The hush over the neighborhood and the sounds of Laura in the kitchen reminded him of Sundays all the way back to his childhood in Chicago. All that was missing was his mother's high soprano voice, who'd used to sing hymn after hymn while she washed dishes on a Sunday. Bill Halsey closed his eyes and like a diver fell headlong into a deep, rapt sleep.

He dreamed that he was joking with Grace Allen, a patient whose visits he had come to dread. She was a nervous spinster teacher in her fifties who cried out at the slightest hint of pain. While he drilled, she held her body stiff and rigid and she gripped the hard arms of her chair so tightly that her long red fingers turned completely white. In his dream he'd finished with Grace Allen. He was walking her out to the front desk, talking a mile a minute. There was a look of relief on her tense face and he was joking with her, nudging her to laugh. He was listening to himself the way he sometimes did, almost appalled by the speeding words which raced out of his mouth like a reckless vehicle that is bound to crash. He was gesticulating and clowning, and Grace Allen was finally laughing, a wilted laugh that sounded more like someone crying. He glanced into the waiting room and there was Lydia Peacham leaning forward in her chair looking at him and at Grace Allen with fascination. She was dressed in pink and her beauty had a radiance that filled the room and burst before Bill Halsey like an explosion. The surprise of seeing her showed in his face.

"I heard you were such a fine dentist, I thought I'd have to come to you myself," she said. She smiled at him, amused, as if she read his thoughts, and in his dream Bill Halsey stuttered and turned red. He fell completely mute. When Lydia sat in the white chair, his mind became as vacant as an empty sky. He searched desperately for words, but nothing came to him that wouldn't sound ridiculous or false. There was music playing on his p.a. system, yet the sound of it did not begin to penetrate the silence of the room. He couldn't even smile. His face was frozen in a mask of frightful seriousness and he felt an overwhelming fear of touching the blonde woman who sat quite calmly waiting for him to begin. She saw the trembling of his hands as he unwrapped the instruments, the awful sweat that stained his shirt and rolled across his forehead, making his glasses slip continually down his nose. Her glowing face tipped back, she watched him coolly while she opened her mouth wide. And when he saw her teeth displayed and shining like a set of brand new pearls, his glasses slipped right off his nose and fell into her startled lap. She jumped. Then with a look of wonder and contempt, she suddenly began to laugh. She laughed and laughed directly in his face, and at that moment in the dream, Bill Halsey fell apart. He dropped his instruments and with a pounding heart he ran out of the room, past his gaping nurse, through the waiting room of staring patients, out the door and down five flights of stairs while the sound of Lydia's laughter followed him in waves and waves that came with a machine-like regularity and frequency until Bill Halsey opened up his eyes and realized that his telephone was ringing. He could hear Laura hurrying up the cellar stairs to answer it.

"It's for you," she said a moment later, coming into the room. "Were you asleep?" She looked surprised. "It's Arthur Varnum."

Bill Halsey held the receiver to his ear and stared at the blurred face in the hall mirror. He'd forgotten to put his glasses on, the ones that had fallen in Lydia Peacham's lap.

"I hate to bother you on a Sunday, Bill," Arthur Varnum was saying. His voice was loud and barking with alertness. "We have a problem. You know about the Johnson family that's staying here at the church?"

"Yes, I read the piece in the Gazette," Bill Halsey said, remembering the article about the homeless family who were camped out in the basement of South Congregational Church. The husband had been laid off from his job in Arkansas over a year ago, and he had driven with his wife and five small children from town to town across the country without finding work. There'd been a photograph of the battered station wagon and the family standing beside it whose hollow-eyed expressions were identical. Even the baby, staring from its mother's arms, had looked grim.

"Jim Johnson has a tooth problem," Arthur Varnum was saying. "He didn't want me to call you, but he's in so much pain, I was hoping there was a chance you might be able to do something for him today. Even if it's just to give him something for the pain. The church will handle the bill. I hate to bother you with this. . ."

"Don't worry about it. I'd be happy to see him," Bill Halsey said, picturing Arthur Varnum's heavy body and his small, sharp eyes protruding with excitement. And between Arthur's bursts of gratitude and blasts of thanks, he managed to arrange to meet Jim Johnson at his office in two hours.

It was close to four when he climbed into his car. He'd changed his clothes and showered, yet his mind was sluggish and his face still pale from sleep. The long, unpleasant dream had changed the mood of the whole day and left him weak and tired.

The light was dim and gentle on the street and he honked at his two daughters who were with a group of children raking leaves. Anne's voice called after him excitely, "Daddy!" but he only waved and kept on going. There wasn't a single tacky building on Main Street where the firehouse, the library and all the little shops made a neat ring around the spotless village green. His daughters, with no memories of ageing brownstone buildings and dingy streets alive with odors, horns and faces, would think of this as home. He pulled into the empty parking lot behind his building, climbed out of his car, and headed toward the street where there wasn't a person or a vehicle in sight. He was aware of the quiet and the sound of his own feet scuffing the hard macadam. As he rounded the corner of the building, he saw Jim Johnson standing by the entrance, his shoulders hunched forward, his hands shoved deep in the pockets of a faded pair of jeans, his weight shifting from foot to foot. There was an awkward and embarrassed look about the man that made Bill Halsey pity him the instant that he saw him. And though it was his rule always to address his patients on a first name basis, he stuck out his hand and said, "You must be Mr. Johnson," as if the formality would reassure and dignify the man.

"Yes, sir," Jim Johnson said, and he wiped his palm on his pants before he shook Bill Halsey's hand. He looked smaller and older than the photography had made him. Bill Halsey guessed that he must be in his early forties, but it was hard to tell. The face was haggard, almost wasted with exhaustion. It was a shocking face, completely ravaged with harsh lines and ridges cut so deep into the skin, Bill Halsey found it painful to look at them. The small blue eyes appeared to dart and struggle in the prison of the face as if they wanted to escape the suffering and misery of it. Bill Halsey was relieved to turn away and fit his key into the lock of the large door.

"It's mighty kind of you to see me on a Sunday," Jim Johnson said behind him. He spoke in a low voice through his nose with a twanging sort of drawl Bill Halsey hadn't heard before.

"No trouble at all," he said, his words reverberating in the empty hallway.

"My teeth are pretty terrible," Jim Johnson said, remaining by the door while the dentist switched the office lights on and the window fan. The air was close and hot, as if the heat were on.

"I was never much for going to the dentist," the man went on in his low voice. His eyes were downcast and Bill Halsey stopped in front of him with the same sense of pity. "There's one or two bad ones in the back, right here," Jim Johnson said, digging a finger into his left cheek. His hair was wild, as if he never combed it and the weather-beaten face looked out of place in the still, modern room. "I'd be mighty grateful if you'd pull them out. I'd just like to be rid of them," he said.

"Well let's have a look at them," Bill Halsey said, leading the man into the smaller room and pointing to the chair.

In his washroom he removed the heavy sweater he was wearing and he put on a clean white jacket, one of several that were hanging in the closet by the sink. He washed his hands, using the brush on his nails, and all the while he was thinking of Jim Johnson's harsh appearance and the powerful way it affected him. He could feel that power now coming through the wall from the man who waited in the chair.

In the past year he hadn't done a single tooth extraction that wasn't prophylactic. People didn't want to lose their teeth these days. They went to specialists for root canals and saved them. His patients were as careful with their mouths as they were with their cars and houses. They came to him at least two times a year to have their teeth cleaned and examined. Most of his work was repair work, replacing dentures and old fillings. There were a good deal of periodontal problems, but he sent most of these patients to Joe Hill across the hall.

As he stood beside the ravaged-looking man, Bill Halsey felt immaculately trim and clean. He set out his gleaming instruments in a row. Jim Johnson's face was not a face he could get used to. Under the bright flourescent light the lines that cut the skin were deeper and more painful, the hair against the headrest was more matted and unruly, and the pallor of the skin was almost ghostly, as if the man were dying of fatigue.

"Let's see what we can do about those teeth," he said, and when he looked into Jim Johnson's mouth, he realized that he hadn't seen a mouth like this since dental school. In those days he had been so anxious to learn all of the techniques that he had hardly noticed anything outside the ruined mouths of those bedraggled men and women who had come to the school in crowds each day for treatment that was cheap and sat the way Jim Johnson now was sitting, unflinching and resigned to pain. Jim Johnson's teeth were stained and crooked, loose or broken. Malocclusion was severe, and there were several missing. He probed and examined every tooth while the man remained entirely motionless and limp against the chair. The left rear molar was decayed down to the nerve, and the one beside it was just as bad. The rancid odor in his face, Bill Halsey straightened up and sighed. "We could save these teeth, but I'd have to send you to another dentist, a friend of mine who's got an office in this building."

"I'd rather you'd pull the both of them out right now," was all that Jim Johnson said with lowered eyes.

"Are you sure?"

The man nodded his head once, sharply, and it seemed to the dentist that there was nothing more to say.

The two teeth were so loose, Bill Halsey hardly had to tug them to extract them. The man, who had refused the novocaine, never showed a sign of pain. When he'd finished, he packed the cheek with gauze, but there was little bleeding. "You can close your mouth," he said.

Jim Johnson opened his eyes. "Are you done?" he asked, and when Bill Halsey nodded, the small blue eyes appeared to come alive in the battered face, and the man, though his cheek bulged with the wad of cotton, smiled broadly with a suddenness that took the dentist by surprise.

"Well thank God," Jim Johnson said profoundly. His voice was loud and energetic, like something risen from the dead. "Those damn teeth were driving me near crazy," he said, looking Bill Halsey in the face. The blue eyes widened and the smile continued. "The past few weeks I swear I couldn't think of nothing but those teeth," he said, and he shook his head, as if the memory of his suffering was amusing to him. Bill Halsey saw that all the hard lines of the face were swept up and obliterated in the smile, and the man appeared transformed. When he stood up from the chair, Jim Johnson looked years younger.

"By damn you're a fine dentist," he said, and he pumped Bill Halsey's hand with a vigorousness that made the dentist feel that the whole of his body had been shaken.

He sent the man ahead of him out of the office and he stayed behind to straighten up the room. But he felt a strange elation and he found himself beside the window, looking down at the street below and waiting for Jim Johnson to appear. The sky was completely dark, the lamps were lit around the village green, and there was an enormous elm which caught the light in all of its yellow leaves and shone above the scene with an eerie brilliance. It came to Bill Halsey that he hadn't laughed or made a single joke in the hour he'd spent with Jim Johnson, and he

94

felt a sweeping and unreasoning happiness at this thought. When he saw the figure of the man below, hurrying across the green, he wanted to open the window and call something to him. But he remained perfectly still with his arms folded tightly over his chest, and he watched Jim Johnson pass under the enormous elm and disappear into the darkness.

Faith

I WAS CHRISTENED Faith Marie after my mother's favorite sister who died of Hodgkin's disease the week before her eighteenth birthday, and whose memory has been preserved with stories of her courage and kindness that always inspired me as a girl. "The good die young," my mother used to sigh whenever she mentioned Auntie Fay, and the saying always worried me. I wanted to be good. It was the one success I could imagine. While I was young, I tried to be as good as I could be, and for as long as my father lived, I gave him little trouble. I was his pride, my mother used to say. If he hadn't died of a stroke in his sleep that Sunday afternoon ten years ago, my life would never have taken the turn it did.

Were mother and father alive today, I know we'd be living just the same as always. We'd be rising at six and retiring at eleven seven days a week. Father would be winning at checkers, gin rummy, and hearts, and mother and I would still be trying to beat him. On Thursday nights we'd eat out at one of the same three restaurants we always went to, and father would be manager of Compton Bank and Trust, where he hardly missed a day for thirty years. Wherever he went, he'd be making a grand impression with the profound conviction of his voice and the power of his penetrating eyes, which could see right into a man. And all the anger in him, which he rarely expressed, would still be stored at the back of his eyes or in the edge of his voice, so that even when he laughed you'd know he wasn't relaxed. He never was relaxed, no matter how he tried. I know I'd be dressed like a proper school girl, conservative and neat in cotton or wool dresses, never pants, my long hair pinned at the sides and rippling down my back or tied up in a braid for church or holidays or dinners out, but never short and boyish the way I wear it now. I'd be odorless and immaculate as ever, without an inkling of a body. And people would still be saying what a graceful girl I was. The way I moved was more like floating. The way I'd walk across our lawn, carrying a frosted glass of mother's minted tea out to the hammock where father read his evening paper in the summer before dinner. Sipping his drink and surveying the mowed yard and trimmed bushes and ever blooming flowers (which were my mother's work), he'd tousle my hair and sigh, "Now this is the life," as if he nearly believed it. Listening to him, I know I'd be as pale as ever, with the face of a girl who lives as much in books as in the world. And I'd feel as far removed from father and that yard as if each page of history or poetry I'd ever read were another mile I'd walked away from home, and each word I learned another door that closed behind me. Though I'd know, no matter what I read, that my mind would never countermand my conscience or overrule my heart. Looking at me, my father's eyes would turn as warm as ever, the way they only seemed to do when he looked at me. Not even at my mother, whose whole mind and heart had been amended, geared to please him, would he ever look that way, without a trace of anger or suspicion. But when he looked at me I'd see the love he never put in words and the faith that I'd never disappoint him. I hoped I never would. To keep the peace, his, my mother's and my own, was such a need I had that had they lived I'm sure the three of us would have passed from Christmas to Christmas, through the dips and peaks of every year, like a ship that's traveling the same circle where the view is always familiar.

I remember one Sunday Father and I were walking home from church all finely dressed and fit to impress whomever we passed. We crossed the green at the center of town and were approached by a pretty girl no more than twenty, who was singing at the top of her voice. She smiled at us as she went by, leaving a strong soprano trill in our ears. I wasn't surprised when Father turned to look at her, outraged. "Now that's the kind of bitch I'd like to see run out of town," he said. I knew he'd say the same to Mother or me if we ever crossed or disappointed him. Because he couldn't tolerate the slightest deviation from his rules. He loved me with all of his heart on the condition that I please him.

Poor Mother couldn't live without Father. He'd been the center of her life for thirty years. Unlike Father, whose beliefs were sacred to him, she had no strong opinions of her own. When he died, she wept with fear as much as grief, as if his death had been a shattering explosion that left our house and town in ruins. She sat all day in his easy chair and couldn't be moved, as if all of her habits as well as her heart were permanently broken. My words and tears never touched her, and it was only two months after Father was gone that she was laid beside him. She was buried in June, the week before our high school graduation.

Compton people who wouldn't speak to me today were concerned and kind when Mother died. There were several families that offered me a home. But I was eighteen, old enough to be on my own, and more at ease in the drawing rooms of novels than I'd ever be in any Compton house. Today there are many in town who believe it was a great mistake, letting me live alone. But I was adamant about it, and I appeared to be as responsible and as mature as any valedictorian of her class is expected to be.

I was as shaken by my parents' death as if the colors of the world had all been changed. Having adjusted myself to my father's wishes for so many years, I had no other inclination. After he was gone, I continued to live exactly as he would have liked me to. If anything, I was more careful than before not to hurt him, as if in death his feelings had become more sensitive than ever and the burden of his happiness was entirely left to me. After Mother's death and the end of school, I took the first available job in town, at Compton library. I was grateful that the work suited me, because I would have taken any job to keep me busy.

Our town of Compton is a tourist town. For three months out of every year the population triples, and Decatur Street is a slow parade of bodies and cars that doesn't end for ninety days. At the end of June, the summer people come. In their enormous yachts and their flashy cars, they arrive. Every year it is a relief to see them come and then a relief to see them go. They are so different from us.

Compton people are short on words. Even in private with their closest kin, the talk is sparse, and actions have more meaning. Whenever Father was troubled, Mother made him a squash pie or one of his other favorites to indicate her sympathy or support. She never asked him to explain. If a man in Compton is well-liked, he'll never have to buy himself a drink at the taverns. By the little favors, by the number of nods he receives on the street, or by the way he is ignored as much as if he were dead, he'll know exactly what his measure is with people. And by the silences, by whether there is comfort or communion in the long pauses between sentences, he'll know exactly how close he is to an acquaintance. I've always known that Compton people were unique. Our women never chattered the way the summer women do, as if there were no end to what they'd say. I've seen the summer people's children awed and muted by the grave reserve and the repressed emotion of a Compton child. And I've seen the staring fascination of all Compton with the open manner of the summer people, who wander through the streets at noon, baring their wrinkled thighs, their cleavage and their bulges to the sun for everyone to see—a people whose feelings flash across their faces as obvious and naked as if they had no secrets. As a child, I used to wander down to watch them at the docks. They seemed as alien and entertaining as a circus troupe. At five o'clock, from boat to boat, there was the sound of ice and glasses, the smell of tonic water, shaving lotion, lipstick and perfume. For evening the women dressed in shocking pink and turquoise, colors bright enough to make a Compton woman blush. There was always laughter interwoven with their conversation, and the liquor made the laughter louder and the talk still freer until the people were leaning into each other's faces or falling into embraces with little cries of "darling" or "my dear." And as I watched them, the gaiety, the confidence, and the warmth of these people always inspired me with affection and yearning for the closeness and the freedom that they knew. It wasn't till I was older I realized

99

that all of their words and embraces brought them no closer to each other than Compton people are—that the distances between them were just as painful and exactly as vast, in spite of the happy illusion they created.

The summer Mother died, I walked to work through the crowds to the rhythm of the cash registers, which never stopped ringing till ten o'clock at night in the restaurants and gift shops all along Decatur Street. And all summer the library, which is a busy place in winter, was nearly empty. I sat at the front desk in the still, dark room, listening to the commotion of cars and voices in the streets. And through the windows I could tell the weather in the patch of sky above the heavy laden elms whose leaves were never still, but trembled, bobbed, and shuddered to every slightest nuance of the air. And seemed to capture and proclaim the whole vitality of every day more truly and completely than any self-afflicted soul could ever hope to render it. I have no other memory of that summer, which disappeared as quickly as it came. But the end of every Compton summer is the same. Even the most greedy merchants are frazzled and fatigued by the daily noise and the rising exuberance of the tourists passing down the coast to home. By then, the beaches and the streets are strewn with cans and papers, as if the town had been a carnival or a zoo, and Compton is glad to see the last of the crowd, whose refuse is only further evidence of the corruption of their pleasure-happy souls.

My first winter alone there were many nights when I cried myself to sleep. I missed my mother's quiet presence in the house and the smells that always rose from the warm, little kitchen where she baked or washed or sat across from me on winter afternoons when I came in from school. Even for a Compton woman she was more than usually quiet, so shy that she had no friends. She went to church on Sunday but the rest of the week she hardly left the yard. My father shopped for all of our food to save her the pain of going out in public. If she'd had her way, she'd never have eaten out with us on Thursday nights. But father insisted on it. "She needs the change," he used to say.

I don't remember Mother ever raising her voice to me in

100

anger. All discipline was left to father. She didn't often kiss or hug me either. But she used to brush my hair one hundred strokes a night, and I remember the gentle touch of her hands. There were times when her shyness made her seem as self-effacing as a nun, and times when I thought I must be living with a saint, the way she read her Bible daily and seemed to have no selfish desires or worldly needs. She dressed in greys and browns, and her dresses hung loose on her bony frame. Though her face was usually serious if not sad, I always believed she was happy in her life with Father and me. She couldn't do enough for us, particularly Father. About her past I only knew that she was born of alcoholic parents who were now both dead, that she'd worshipped her sister, Faith, and that she never corresponded with her other sister, Mary, who lived in California and was also alcoholic. Most often Mother didn't like to reminisce. If I asked her a question she didn't like, she didn't answer it. There were some weeks when she spoke so little that if she hadn't read aloud to me, I hardly would have heard her voice. It was her reading aloud at night that I missed the most after she was gone. It was a habit we kept from before I could read to myself, when to hear her speak page after page was a luxury as soothing and as riveting as any mystery unravelling itself to revelation. It was through the sound of her voice speaking someone else's words that I knew my mother best.

That first winter I cried many nights with all the fear and passion of the child I was and would ever have remained had I been given a choice. And, with a child's love, I saw the images of my father and mother rise up in the dark above my bed as clear and painfully defined as the impression they had left upon my heart. I cried also for the simplicity of my old life. The simple life of a child who wants to please. For I recognized myself among the spinster women of our town, of whom there are many. Women who never leave the houses of their stern fathers and their silent, sacrificing mothers, houses of a kind so prevalent in Compton. Daughters with all of the rebellion driven out of them at an early age, all of the rudeness skimmed away, severely lashed and molded by the father's anger and the mother's fear of all the changing values in the sinful world. Many of our Compton spinsters are sensitive, high strung. You can see they were the children who avoided pain, preferred endearments and affection. They rarely gossip the way the married women do. To their mothers and their fathers they are faithful and devoted to the end, loyal to the present and the past, forgetful of the future. So much I see about them now that I didn't know when I counted myself one of them.

I had one friend from childhood, Mary Everly, who was studying to be a nurse in a city fifty miles away. Though she sometimes wrote to me, she never came home, finding Compton a "stifling" place. I was close to no one else in town. A few months after Mother died, the invitations to supper and the concerned calls from neighbors stopped. Like my mother, I was shy. I had no skill at small talk and was relieved to be left in peace. But I analyzed myself the way a lonely person wonders why he is not loved. And I studied my life until I was as far removed from it as if I had been carved and lifted out of Compton and left to hover like a stranger over everything familiar.

Two times I went to visit Father Ardley in his blue-walled office at the vestry, and twice the touch of his thumb on my forehead, where he signed the cross, brought me to tears. I was drawn to the love of the church. I had an unexamined faith in God, but a fear that His demands would be crushing, were I to take them to heart. It was an irrational fear I tried to explain to Father Ardley, whose eyes were as cold as a winter sky while his voice was like the sun warming it. "You are still in mourning, Faith," he said to me. "Such a loss as you've suffered can't be gotten over quickly. You must pray to God and keep yourself busy, child," he said, though I had never been idle in my life, not ever, then or now.

For seven years I was as busy as I could be. My conscience kept me well supplied with tasks, and there is no end to what a person ought to do. I worked at the library. I lived in my father's house. I baked for the church bazaars. I visited Father Ardley. The summer people came and left as regularly as the tides. I had as many warm acquaintances as ever, and I had no close friends.

I still wrote letters to Mary Everly, who was now a nurse, married, and living in Cincinnati with her second baby on the way. Though the memory of my parents' love sustained me, and my father's wishes continued to guide me, time diluted their power to comfort me. Some mornings, walking through the sunny streets to work, the thought of death would take me by surprise, and I knew that mine would mean no more to anyone in town than the sudden disappearance of a picket fence on Elm Street or a missing bed of flowers in Gilbey Park.

I never went out with men. Not that I wasn't attractive. My father used to tell me I was pretty, and Mrs. Beggin at the library said I was a "lovely looking girl" and she couldn't see why I wasn't married yet. But Compton men knew different. Something they saw behind my shyness frightened them away. Something my mother and father had never seen. For beneath it all I wasn't a normal Compton woman, not typical no matter how I tried to be. Whether it was the influence of the summer people or the hours I had escaped in books, I was always "different" as far as Compton men could see, and they were just as strange to me.

It was the eighth summer after mother's death that I met Billy Tober. I was just twenty-six. William Tober IV, his family had named him. He was a summer boy, four years younger than I, a college student, though his eyes were the shallow blue of a flier's or a sailor's. I noticed him before he ever noticed me. I'd always see him with a different girl with the same smile on his lips. He began to come to the library many afternoons. He liked poetry and novels, and he'd ask me for suggestions. I was surprised when he began to appear at the end of the day to walk me home. It wasn't long before we began to meet in the evenings too.

I wish I could say that I remember Billy well, and I wish that I could describe him clearly. But I can't remember much that he ever said and barely how he looked. I only remember the effect he had upon me. As if I knew how it would end, I never invited him to my house, and I'd only allow him to walk me halfway home, which made him laugh at first. In the evening, I'd meet him at Gilbey Park, which is just outside the center of Compton.

It is a pretty hill of bushes, trees, and flowers which overlooks the harbor. On a hidden bench we sat and sipped the wine that Billy always brought. Though I'd never tasted liquor or sat and talked with a young man, I was completely at ease. The wine and the dusky out-of-doors loosened my tongue until my hidden thoughts rose up as urgently as if my life depended on telling them. It often surprised me what I said, because whenever I was with Billy I was a different woman, so unlike my usual self I'm sure no one in Compton would have recognized me. It was as natural as breathing, the way I'd change into a giddy girl whenever I was with him. "Where did you ever get such hair?" he asked about the curls my mother never let me cut. After that, it was my eyes he noticed. My neck was regal as a queen's, he said. And there was pride as well as grace in the way I walked. My hands, the smallness of my waist, my legs, my voice he also praised. I couldn't hear enough. For the month of July we saw each other every night. At home, I'd often stare for an hour at the stranger in the mirror, this woman with a body that a man desired.

Whatever it is that attracts a man to a woman I've too little experience to know. But I believe that for Billy every woman was a challenge. He was as restless and driven a person as I've known. Obsession with a woman must have soothed him. He used to tell me that he loved me, but I'm sure that if he'd heard the same from me, his feelings would have died. If I'd loved him, I would have told him. He begged me often enough to say it. But I never was able to. "We're too different," I insisted. "I'm not myself when I'm with you." But I gloried in the power he'd given me. I was in love with his desire, which singled me out from all the world and made the world a painless kingdom where I ruled the more he wanted me. We met most nights in August. We drove out to Haskall Beach to a private place I knew. By then we hardly spoke, and there were times, with his breath hot on my face and his voice crying my name, I felt I'd be more comforted and serene if I were sitting there alone and free of all the yearning human arms can cause.

All those nights we spent together, I never took precautions. "Is it safe?" he asked me many times. But I ignored the question, as if it would have been the crowning sin if I'd been careful to prevent any meaning or possibility of love to come out of the fire of vanity and ignited pride which burned between us. Driving back to town, the silence in the car was so oppressive that it taunted us.

The day that Billy left, I felt relieved, and in the weeks that followed, I didn't miss him once, which surprised me. We wrote no letters to each other. Life went back to normal, and the longer he was gone the more I began to hope I'd never see him again.

When doctor Filser told me I was pregnant, I could see he was surprised the way all Compton would be. I saw the way he looked at me with new, appraising eyes, and I burned to think of all the other eyes that would be privy to scenes of Billy and me on Haskall Beach. For I knew they'd piece it all together down to every detail.

When I told Father Ardley the news, I aimed the words and threw them at him one by one like darts. But his tone was not what I expected. He wasn't angry with me. "I suppose it was that summer boy you were seeing," he sighed, and he knew enough not to suggest the marriage he'd have insisted upon had Billy Tober been a Compton boy. Instead, he gave me the name of Brighton Adoption Agency.

For all of the nine months I carried the child as if it were a sin beyond forgiveness and there was no forgetting or ignoring it. I felt my father's wrath in every room of the house, and I never visited his or my mother's grave, knowing the affront it would be. As if they'd died again, I felt bereft. I was sure they wanted no part of me now and that I could never turn to them again.

Compton people were not so harsh. As much as they disapproved, they also pitied me. No one tried to deprive me of my job. Though there were some who would no longer speak to me, there were more whose pity moved them to be kinder than before. My humiliation was enough for them and lesson enough for their children. When they saw that my cross was sufficiently heavy, they approved. Even now, times when my heart is light and I'm tempted to laugh in public, I check myself. I know I'll always be on good behavior in Compton, and the more abject I appear, the better off I'll be.

It is ten o'clock, the last day of May, a Saturday, and all of the windows in the house are open for the first time this season. There is a cold breeze coming off the harbor, running through the rooms in currents that break against the walls and boil the curtains halfway to the ceiling. Every year it is the same, the day of opening the windows. The sea wind scours every corner of the house until its heavy atmosphere is broken. All of the memories which hang in odors are borne away until the rooms are only rooms and this woman, dreaming at a littered kitchen table, is as relieved as if she'd just received communion, left all of her habits at the altar rail, and returned to her pew with no identity but her joy.

It is so quiet. The baby is asleep upstairs under a pink quilt. When he wakes, he will have roses in his cheeks. He is so blond, his hair is nearly white. He bears no likeness to my family, and yet the night he was born I knew he was mine as surely as these arms or thoughts belong to me. After the pain of labor, as if I had been delivered of all shame, I asked to see the child. When I saw two waving arms, a tiny head, my heart rose up, amazed. And when they put him in my arms, it was love I held, all warmly wrapped, alive.

So many tired-looking mothers you see in Compton. They hardly seem to care how they appear. Wearing shabby clothes, herding their little broods across the streets, worried and snapping orders at them. But a Compton woman never shows her deepest feelings to the world. When Paul was first at home, I used to kiss his little face at least a hundred times a day. Who but an infant or God could stand so much affection? And all of those kisses were just the beginning of love, the first expression of my newly seeded heart which bloomed, expanded, and flowered with every kiss.

At five o'clock I'd pick the baby up from Mrs. Warren who cared for him the hours I worked. We'd ride home on a crowded bus of Compton women in their fifties, carefully dressed, who rested their heavy bodies behind a row of shopping bags. When they saw the child, their eyes grew soft and bright. "What a love," they'd say, all smiles, and they'd ask his name or age and touch the corner of his blanket so gingerly, with reverence, as if they had forgotten all of the strain, the distraction, the heavy weight of care which had exalted them and only remembered how close they once had come to perfect love. I could see them in their kitchens years ago, bathing their babies in the little plastic tubs that Compton mothers use. I could imagine them, once so shy and bending to the will of the town, their fathers, and their husbands, becoming fierce and stubborn, demanding so much satisfaction, comfort, and such happiness for their little ones as they had never dreamed of for themselves.

By now I ought to have the kitchen clean, the wash brought in and folded, and the vegetables picked and washed. It is so rare I sit and dream that when I do the memories come fast and heavy as an avalanche. I've known some cynics who remember only pain and ugliness, as if the way a man remembers corresponds with what he hopes. When Paul was born, it changed my past as well as the future. Now, when I look back, I see beauty. The older the memory, the more beautiful it has become. Even moments of great pain or disappointment have been transformed, given an importance and a dignity they never had at the time, as if whatever happens and wherever I have failed may one day be redeemed in the far future. I pray it will be so.

Perfection

IF IT WERE POSSIBLE, I'd lead you out of this room to another room or similar moment. Above a quiet meal, beside a candle, I'd have you repeat what you were saying. Your idea was so beautifully put it took my breath away. But Polly wouldn't let you finish. She interrupted you at nearly every word and fractured the spell you almost cast till I could barely preserve your little portrait of a native (was it North African?) who when he looked at a tree, looked at it differently than we do. For him an ugly tree did not exist, you said. All trees, no matter what they looked like, whatever their age or size, were perfect, just as all things were to him perfect creations. I saw him standing on a perfect hill under a perfect sky looking out of a perfect body at a perfect view, never saying to a friend, "Oh, what a beautiful tree." And I had a violent longing to push my hand across the forbidden territory of Polly's face, who talks so much she never hears, who if she were a Christian and Christ himself appeared, would argue with him about church doctrine without a bit of awe. Tonight she is as annoying as a tooth ache. The evening is galloping on and you are just about to leave the table.

Why haven't you gone already? I may never know. You and I always settle for the surface, like people who think a poem is destroyed if it is dissected or discussed too much, though I've never understood people like that, how, worshipping mystery, they can ever marry or want to follow any subject to the end, when they seem to believe that the truth on close inspection is always ugly. But my own mind is contradictory. Right now, for instance, what if you were to urge me, though we aren't lovers or close friends, to sit on your lap with my head resting on your shoulder, arms around you, lips just touching your neck? I can imagine it so well. Very softly I'd say in your ear, "If all the clothes I change and wear and wash, if everything I do passes through my conscious sieve, leaving only a residue later called nostalgia, and all is changing and nothing predictable, how absurd it must be to ask me my opinion of anything, my opinion of my mother, or the weather, or anything which, having known it, I would have loved, disliked, held as many opinions as there are words. And if I must accept the fact that my judgment will always be faulty, is it any wonder I wanted to cling to your vision of a native looking at a tree, who, while I can't comprehend him, must seem like a super-human seer?" Barely knowing you, is it conceivable that I could, without your thinking I was being seductive, sit on the floor while you sit in your chair, and put my head in your lap? Just because it would be perfection, which may always only be momentary.

I wonder why people ever speak at all, when everything they say is barely an outline, and no one is interesting or important enough to hold any audience for long. But what if you could never have enough of me? Or what if a man sat with a woman and said, "Tell me about yourself," leaning back in his chair, looking alert yet so relaxed it seemed he had no house to go home to, no job, and no future demands at all? What if he said, "Tell me what you think about things," settled back without even a cigarette or a drink to separate them? She, nonplussed, seeing he really might be serious, could fall completely mute, as if she had suddenly been handed a microphone, unable to believe he could really want to know. After all, what was so important about her lifetime? And if neither of them had a sex or any vanity, would they even bother to say hello as they passed each other on the street? But putting all of this aside, burdened with a sudden ton of experience and a chance to exist, she might half-laughing, maybe slightly embarrassed but mustering up her dignity, begin to speak. At first, with gratitude, she would keep her sentences short, and there would be no digressions. She would try to please, her tone of voice lively, embellished with graceful faces and gestures. Sometimes silence makes the heart grow fonder, she would know, pausing politely at the end of each clipped paragraph to wait for some encouragement. But each time, if she found him still fascinated, she might be tempted to say, "I think I'll tell you a long, involved story," just to test him. And if his eyes hadn't wandered from her face and his brain were a boat whose movements she could direct, then she could go on. Turning to the third person, more dignified and refreshing that a continuous "I," and changing the sex of her protagonist for added interest, she would begin her tale. Once I had a friend who knew exactly what he wanted. When he was twenty-two, he took me for a drive one day fifteen miles out of the city to show me his dream house. If I never own it, I'll never be happy, he said. But he didn't appear to be gloomy, even though the young couple that owned the place had several children, dogs and cats, and appeared to be settled down to a long life in the vine-covered Victorian cottage. I've told them what the house means to me, he said as we drove off. And they've promised to contact me if they ever decide to sell.

When he was twenty-eight, my friend still gave himself good odds for happiness in spite of his unbending demands and rigid needs. He had a job that was satisfying to him. He had friends. He still did not own his dream house, but he had a large savings. If the house went up for sale, he'd not only be able to buy it, but furnish it as well, exactly to the plan he'd already drawn up for every room. "But all of this is superfluous," he said to me. "The thing that haunts me is the woman that I want to marry. I haven't found her yet, though I know just what she looks like and how she dresses. I can hear her voice, what the tone of it would be," he said. "I know that I'll recognize her the moment that I see her. Sometimes I stand on sidewalks near restaurants or shops or museums I think she might visit, just waiting for her."

When I said to my friend, as I often did, that I thought he was cracked, probably the maddest person I had ever known, he smiled. "But to change my taste would be like trying to change the shape of my head or the length of my arms, wouldn't it?" he asked. He was desperate. His affairs with women had been infrequent and unsatisfying. That he had never been in love tortured him. Yet his pursuit of his fantasy lady, who stood in the way of all others, continued, and became more frantic every year, until it was evident to his friends that he was no longer a charming eccentric but a hardened neurotic whose infantile obsession needed a psychiatric cure. He submitted to the advice of everyone he knew. But after four years of analysis, his dream was still intact, and he resumed the search for his wife, as he always called her, with a determination that was more grim than ever. Two summers he spent in Europe and Australia, and two summers he combed the United States from coast to coast without finding her.

Here, at the apex of her story, the woman might pause to catch her breath or wait for further encouragement or to luxuriate a bit before relinquishing her spell. And her snared listener, nettled and impatient would be bound to cry, "Well, what happened? Did he ever find her?"

"Yes," she would begin again, and she would speak slowly, basking in her conclusion, like a cat lying on a window sill delighting in the sun. "It was extraordinary. To the amazement of his friends, he did. He was thirty-four, at a New Year's party, just about to leave as he often did as soon as he'd looked over the crowd, when she arrived. There are a number of stories about what actually happened. Some people insist that he hadn't even seen her face, that she was standing in her hat and coat with her back to him when he turned pale, left a conversation in the middle of a sentence, walked across to her, put both hands on her shoulders, and turned her gently to face him. No one knows what he said to her. But they stood for several moments, he still with his hands on her shoulders, once taking her chin and tipping up her face while he spoke, she a little surprised but making no effort to move. Everyone in the room who knew him knew what was happening, saw a kind of rapture and disbelief come into the face of the dark-haired girl who stood, still in her coat, snow still on her hair and shoulders, long arms hanging helpless at her sides, the room full of people and her husband, a young doctor who stood nearby speaking with the hostess, forgotten. They looked like lovers, oblivious, and his triumph reflected in her face and over the whole glowing room. Later, when she was reclaimed by her trembling husband and whisked away in tears, my friend was surrounded by anxious acquaintances who expected the worst. They were surprised. That his dream wife was married to someone else seemed not to faze him in the least. He celebrated until dawn. That the girl existed and that his passion for her was real appeared to be enough for him. He never tried to see her again, not wanting to upset her life, he said. He lost interest in the Victorian cottage and six months later was happily married to someone else."

Here the woman might stop speaking. After all, she would have to stop sometime. And really, wouldn't she only have spoken as long as it seemed worth her while? If she weren't attracted to her listener, if he aroused in her no sympathy or excitement and if she didn't want him to love, admire, or desire her, why bother to go on? And why bother with a man whose very willingness to listen on and on must seem a weakness. Had he no motives or any future? Why, it would be a waste of time, and she would grow bored with herself and her stories and ideas, just the way people don't follow their own silent thoughts too far alone in their heads unless these thoughts have some connection to a driving need or purpose in the world. This might be why, aside from any fear, you and I are often silent when we're together, not knowing whether there is any reason we should speak.

One final thing I think, waiting for you to look at me before you leave, remembering how strange it is that eyes can say so much. They have told me more than words or bodies have. I've never known rage, joy, terror, or death depicted better than by eyes. They are like an ever changing haiku, a brief, brilliant summation of the whole person and the whole moment. It's things like eyes that make me believe in perfection, because there is no getting away from the truth of them. I think of your eyes when they grow soft and warm, the way your whole expression, normally so closed and stiff, blossoms. I've noticed this, and it's sad the way I often equate a completely open and excited face looking full into mine with sex. Sad because the intimacy that eyes can promise is often more than sex can fulfill.

I wish we were just finishing a lively conversation that left us both refreshed, or that you would ask me at least one question before you leave. But I'm a fearful dreamer. I've read that people deprived of their dreams become quickly psychotic. I've also read that the most enlightened man never dreams, and if he does, he thinks it a bad sign.

Your face is an assault of smiling reservations, an unenlightened but intelligent face, like my own, best able to express its most enduring conviction in sleep.